FORTY DAYS PLUS THREE
Daily Reflections for Lent and Holy Week

FORTY DAYS PLUS THREE

Daily Reflections for Lent and Holy Week

John J. McIlhon

THE LITURGICAL PRESS
Collegeville, Minnesota 56321

Cover by Joshua Jeide, O.S.B.

Nihil obstat: Rev. Lawrence A. Beeson, J.C.D., *Censor deputatus.*
Imprimatur: ✝ William H. Bullock, D.D., Bishop of Des Moines, December 28, 1988.
Excerpts from the English translation of non-biblical readings from *The Liturgy of the Hours* © 1974, International Committee on English in the Liturgy, Inc. All rights reserved.

ISBN 0-8146-1769-7

		4	5	6	7	8	9	10

Library of Congress Cataloging-in-Publication Data

McIlhon, John.
    Forty days plus three : daily reflections for Lent and Holy Week / by John J. McIlhon.
        p.   cm.
    ISBN 0-8146-1769-7
    1. Lent—Meditations. 2. Holy Week—Meditations.   I. Title.
BV85.M38   1989
242'.34—dc19
                          88-35693
                          CIP

Contents

Preface

"I wish there was a way that a mother of twelve kids could have Lent at home with her."

This was the wishful thinking of my sister-in-law, Raymetta McIlhon, as we shared a pot of coffee one afternoon and anticipated the return of seven of her twelve "kids" from school. Her wish intrigued me. I must admit, however, that since then it has been on the back burner of my things to do for a very long time. This book is evidence that I finally brought Raymetta's suggestion up to the front burner for those who might like to celebrate Lent both at home and in church.

The source from which I wrote this book is volume 2 of *Liturgy of the Hours*. For those who obligate themselves to the daily mission of praying with the universal Church, this is the Church's "way" of taking the mysteries of Christ's life outside the portals of churches, where the liturgy of prayer and worship is also at home. This book was written as I pondered each day's Office of Readings in my home during the 1986 Lenten season. Later, it occurred to me that I had at hand the fulfillment of my sister-in-law's wish.

Each chapter of this book contains three parts: "Word," "Reflection," and "Questions for Your Reflection." "Word" highlights Office of Readings excerpts taken from *Liturgy of the Hours*. "Reflection" is the fruit of my discernment of the readings for insights apropos of our time. "Questions for Your Reflection" was designed to invite readers to prayerful discernment for their own insights amidst Lent's inexhaustible treasures of Scripture and tradition, abundant in the Church's universal prayer.

A word about "Questions for Your Reflection." It is not my intention that all of the questions be answered each day. One question each day will suffice as inducement to prayer. Leave some of the questions for other Lents.

Each of us is Christ's sanctuary, wherever we are. This book was not written, however, to invite abandonment of our church sanctuaries where Christ's Lenten mysteries are celebrated. Rather, it was written for those who long to take Lent's mysteries of faith with them wherever they go. Indeed, God is in our churches. I hope this book will remind us that God is also everywhere!

John J. McIlhon

Foreword

Some appropriately describe the Lenten season as a spiritual journey. I see the forty-day trek as a pilgrimage. On a pilgrimage we never travel alone. Pilgrims travel in groups; they become a community. In our Lenten walk we move from Ash Wednesday to Easter Sunday not alone but with others who search for a renewed relationship with the Risen Savior. The community walks together.

Two images come to mind about Lent: the first picture is that of a nomadic tribe of freed slaves wandering forty years in the Sinai Desert on pilgrimage to the promised land. The second image is that of Jesus himself in the desert, praying and fasting for forty days and forty nights prior to the beginning days of his public ministry. These images mirror two realities in our own lives. Joined in the community of the Church with one another, we are the new testament people of God, living as in a desert, in journeying together to the Father. But there is a significant difference. We know our goal and we know the way. Our destiny is that heavenly city "with foundations whose designer and maker is God" (Heb 11:11). And our way is Christ Jesus, who is "the Way, the Truth, and the Life" (John 14:6).

Unfortunately on our pilgrimage these landmarks do not lessen the barrenness of "the world"—that spirit which is antithetical to God. Mirages of pleasure tempting us to worship "the creature rather than the creator" (Rom 1:25) are ever present. And we are often tested to see if we will rely on bread alone, rather than on "every word that comes from the mouth of God" (Matt 4:4).

Lent teaches us some foundational lessons. Apart from the Church, from the manna of Eucharist and community among God's people, we are liable to death. True Christians don't live in isolation from one another. Lent invites us to feed on the manna of Christ. It bids us join forces with one another in the solidarity of the Spirit. Lent is a time

9

for us to blend our voices in common prayer, to join our hands in communion with all members of the Body of Christ.

Lent also shows us Christ himself in greater clarity. He is the pillar of fire by night to which we must look when faith alone is our guide. He is the rock that gives us the living water of the Spirit. He is that manna from heaven given to us by the Father who gives to the one who asks "as much as that person needs" (Luke 11:8). The foundational concepts of Christ and Christian community as essentials for the pilgrim are masterfully embodied in *Forty Days Plus Three: Daily Reflections for Lent and Holy Week*. Our author, Monsignor John McIlhon, has combined readings from the communal prayer of the Church—the Liturgy of the Hours—with private reflection. He joins the richness of these readings contemplated during Lent by the whole Church with provoking and challenging meditations. Monsignor McIlhon stretches us to think and pray not alone but in concert with "the whole Christ" (St. Augustine), coupling the Lenten readings with provoking questions to mind and heart. His meditations beautifully reference the Church's continued teaching through the Second Vatican Council, beckoning the pilgrim to move forward toward Easter.

The centerpiece of this Lenten *vademecum* is that of Genesis 1: each person is created in the image and likeness of God. Sin is portrayed as a tarnishing of that image, of betrayal of the identity announced in this first book of the Bible. With the skill of an artist, Monsignor McIlhon creates the centerpiece by washing his canvas with variegated colors. His unique style and fresh ideas invite the reader to explore the image of God in oneself from different angles. Such reflections systematically prepare the pilgrim to discover renewed relationship with the Risen Christ in the Lenten passage.

The author has composed these Lenten reflections not only out of his wide acquaintance with the spiritual Masters but also from an intensive personal experience of the struggle and growth that occurs only in personal life's deserts. His convincing insistence on the dignity of the human person springs from an ownership of his own redeemed self in Christ. He calls us to explore our own definition of self-worth vis-a-vis that worth ascribed to us by the world. He challenges us to eschew those measures too often accepted by us from our culture—our possessions and status. His book is not only a special work; it is a personal witness to Christ in his own priestly life.

It is precisely from these hollow external values that the author points to the solid internal reality of our created and redeemed being.

We are created in God's image and likeness. We are called to share God's life as his most beloved children. We are invited to live "the law of the Spirit, the Spirit of life in Christ Jesus, who has freed us from the law of sin and death" (Rom 8:2).

These meditations are meant to be read with the eyes of faith. The thoughts and words of this book will penetrate our hearts according to the measure of our openness to the Spirit. With a prayer to the Holy Spirit before reading, and with a few moments for quiet reflection thereafter, the Pillar of Fire will become perceptible, drawing the pilgrim forward to the celebration of Easter.

Finally, there is a bit of Irish wisdom captured in a hymn once recorded by tenor John McCormick. It is about how to live with difficulties and suffering. "O barren gain and bitter loss" . . . until at last we learn "to kiss the cross."

In this insightful meditation for the great season of Lent, Monsignor John McIlhon reflects on the wisdom of this greatest of stories: the death and resurrection of Jesus.

His reflection reveals the lived faith of one who has personally appropriated the wisdom of the paschal mystery. I highly recommend *Forty Days Plus Three: Daily Reflections for Lent and Holy Week.* And I will use these meditations to enrich my own Lent.

> Most Reverend William H. Bullock, D.D.
> Bishop of Des Moines

But What About God's Longing?

WORD

"This is the fasting I wish:
releasing those bound unjustly,
untying the thongs of the yoke;
Setting free the oppressed,
breaking every yoke;
Sharing your bread with the hungry,
sheltering the oppressed and the homeless;
Clothing the naked when you see them,
and not turning your back on your own" (Isa 58:6-7).

REFLECTION

Ash Wednesday again! Millions of people flock to their churches to receive ashes. They hear a call to repent. They are invited to fast, pray, and give alms. This is concrete. This is something they can handle. They pledge that they will fast, pray, and give alms during Lent.

People are sincere about keeping their resolve. But let's face it. Easter will come, and, alas, things will be the same. Other than the satisfaction that they have been fairly faithful to their Lenten exercises, there really won't be a noticeable change. There will still be found wanting the deep peace they hoped fasting, prayer, and almsgiving would bring.

The problem, I suggest, is that too often we begin Lent with secondary longings. We long for *our* peace; we long for *our* opportunity to forgive or be forgiven; we long to have *our* wounds healed; we long to be rid of *our* addictions; we long to have others understand *us;* we long to be taken seriously by those *we* seriously love. These are authentic longings, and God truly takes them seriously. But are they primary?

13

There is one more longing we need to consider at the beginning of Lent—a longing crucial to the renewal that makes repentance effective and felt. What about God's longing? Deeper than all of our longings is God's longing that the poor be treated justly and with dignity. This is the longing that gives meaning to fasting, prayer, and almsgiving. Our ascetical practices are not claim checks we hand to God on Easter Sunday to verify the achievement of Ash Wednesday resolutions. Fasting, prayer, and almsgiving are, rather, the indispensable means at our disposal for discerning the longing of God.

When there is a call to turn back to God, there is a call to turn to the poor. Why? Because that's where God is. God longs to be found with the poor because they are the ones who verify that injustice exists. It is imperative that those who have the goods of this world see clearly that what makes for righteousness is not what people have but who people are. God is with the poor to verify that human dignity, not earthly possessions, is everyone's claim to righteousness. We fast from the things we have so that we might see more clearly God's longing in behalf of human dignity. Christ's presence among the poor is God's judgment not to condemn the rich but to condemn the dignity the rich very often attribute to worldly possessions.

Let us not, however, limit the poor to those who are deprived of food, clothing, or shelter. The poor are all who are forced to live in conditions of indignity and injustice. Some of the poorest of the poor are those who are our closest associates and companions—a parent, a child, a grandparent, a fellow worker, a teacher, a student, the boy who bags our groceries. It may be an elderly neighbor whose telephone has not rung for days. It may be the parish priest who places the ashes on our heads at the Ash Wednesday liturgy.

What is the fasting God wants? It is a fasting that corresponds to God's longing: "releasing those bound unjustly, untying the thongs of the yoke; setting free the oppressed, breaking every yoke; sharing your bread with the hungry, sheltering the oppressed and the homeless; clothing the naked when you see them, and not turning your back on your own" (see "Word" above).

Yes, we all begin Lent with deep, deep longings. Perhaps we need to fast from our longings and focus on the longing of God. With such repentance, we "shall call, and the LORD will answer, [we] shall cry for help, and [God] will say, 'Here I am!' " (Isa 58:9)

QUESTIONS FOR YOUR REFLECTION

1. Are you afraid to listen to God as the Spirit tries to tell you what God longs to bring about in your life?

2. What person living closest to you is poor?

3. Excluding material possessions, what is your poverty?

4. Is there, for you, a relationship between questions two and three? If so, does question one shed some light?

THURSDAY AFTER ASH WEDNESDAY

Lent's Centerpiece

WORD

"The special note of the paschal feast is this: the whole Church rejoices in the forgiveness of sins" (St. Leo the Great).[1]

REFLECTION

Whenever we fail to identify the centerpiece of any undertaking, we complicate our endeavors. It is this complexity that discourages us and causes us to give up.

Lent's centerpiece is the forgiveness of sins. "The special note of the paschal feast is this: the whole Church rejoices in the forgiveness of sins" (see "Word" above). The reason forgiveness is the centerpiece of Lent is that forgiveness is the centerpiece of Christ's love and our response to that love. But forgiveness is possible only when we admit that another sovereignty has occupied the center of our lives. It ought not go unnoticed that the first person to whom Jesus appeared after his resurrection was Mary Magdalene. She was re-owned by Christ because she no longer claimed the strange gods of her past as the centerpiece of her life.

When St. Leo suggests that the special note of Easter is the forgiveness of sins, he is likewise suggesting that the special note of Lent is the daily process whereby we gradually purify ourselves of an enslavement to the sovereignty of sin, which is the essence of all sinfulness. "Sin is sin," said a little child, "because 'I' is in the middle of it." The essence of sin is not sinful thoughts, words, or deeds as such. Sin's evil lurks in the attitudes of persons who seek lordship by means of the very thoughts, words, and deeds that God created to be the instruments that express participation in the life of God.

Forgiveness is not a good feeling that an evil smudge has been wiped away from our souls. Rather, forgiveness consists in a restored relationship to the God who is the meaning of life's wholeness and who seeks to be identified with that wholeness. Conversion consists in the renunciation of all peership with God and the re-owning of the creaturehood that is truly our honor and glory. Forgiveness arises from the conviction that creation is good not because it can be sovereign but because it is creaturely and, in that creatureliness, eligible to mediate the grandeur of God.

Lent is the time to renew this perspective. We fast and give alms not because these have been arbitrarily designated by some juridic decree as the official Lenten asceticism. Rather, fasting and almsgiving release us from the captivity of our illusions of grandeur. It is by means of these ascetical practices that we begin to gain a renewed sense of our creaturehood, enabling us to see all of God's creation not as commodities for our aggrandizement but as gifts from a loving creator to creatures created to share in God's image and likeness.

We begin Lent acknowledging that we have become slaves to the lie that created goods can make us like God. We choose an asceticism of prayer, fasting, and almsgiving that we might be liberated from this delusion. Forgiveness is the restoration of God's status as creator and our status as children of that creator. This restoration is the centerpiece of Lent's work and Easter's glory. Dying to the illusions of creatorship, we are raised up to the glory of a creaturehood that enables God's creatorship to unfold the creator's glory within the endless depths of creaturehood's mystery.

QUESTIONS FOR YOUR REFLECTION

1. What occupies most of your thoughts throughout each day?

2. What do you talk about each day when you are with people you like?

3. How do you spend your spare money?

4. Based on answers to the above questions, what is the centerpiece of your life? Is there a need for forgiveness to occupy Lent's center position?

Prayer: Longing to See Christ

WORD

"Pharaoh's daughter . . . was moved to pity for him and said, 'It is one of the Hebrews' children.' Then his sister asked Pharaoh's daughter, 'Shall I go and call one of the Hebrew women to nurse the child for you?' 'Yes, do so,' she answered" (Exod 2:5-8).

"Our spirit should be quick to reach out toward God, not only when it is engaged in meditation; at other times also when it is carrying out its duties, caring for the needy, performing works of charity, giving generously in the service of others" (St. John Chrysostom, bishop).[2]

REFLECTION

The author of the Epistle to the Hebrews touches the meaning of prayer: "Let us keep our eyes fixed on Jesus" (Heb 12:2). Prayer is not finely crafted words or lofty thoughts offered to God. Rather, prayer is a deep longing, like hunger and thirst, to see God. That longing is but the echo of God's own deep longing to share eternal life with us: "Give glory to your Son . . . that he may bestow eternal life on those you gave him" (John 17:1-2).

But where do we see God? St. John writes: "No one has ever seen God" (1 John 4:12). True, none of us has ever seen God in the same way that we see earthly realities. Nevertheless, if we long to care for the needs of our brothers and sisters, we are as close to seeing God as is possible on this earth. Those who hunger and thirst to fix their

17

eyes on the poor are revealing the fruits of prayer. Prayer always leads to justice, which relishes the perfection of human dignity. Christ dwells in the perfection of that dignity. "God dwells in us, and his love is brought to perfection in us" (1 John 4:12).

St. Thomas Aquinas suggests that whatever is received is received according to one's capacity to receive it. If I am able to appropriate a new idea to my personhood, it will be in terms of some frame of reference within my experience. George Gershwin, for example, wrote his "Rhapsody in Blue" as a serious piece of music. Serious musicians, however, initially rejected his music because jazz seemed to them not to be within the range of the classics.

It is prayer's purpose to form us to be received by God as God created us to become. God created us to be human that in our creaturehood we might be readied to receive God as God truly is. Our capacity to receive God is a human, graced capacity. It is prayer's purpose to ready us for the presence of God through the prism of Jesus' human nature. To fix our eyes on Jesus, then, we must be ready to fix our eyes on those incarnational realities where Jesus truly dwells, not where we imagine he dwells.

Prayer sheds light on the poor that we might have the capacity to discern the presence of the Lord in their midst. Prayer is light bringing to light the conviction that Jesus is exactly where he said he would be: "As often as you did it for one of my least [ones] you did it for me" (Matt 25:40). St. John Chrysostom writes: "Our spirit should be quick to reach out toward God not only when it is engaged in meditation [but] also when it is carrying out its duties, caring for the needy, performing works of charity, giving generously in the service of others" (see "Word" above).

Prayer's longing is not for a God who ignores the historical circumstances of people's lives. Authentic prayer leads us into the very center of history. God is as close to us today in the circumstances of our history as God was in the circumstances experienced by Moses' frightened sister, who watched as he slept nearby in a papyrus basket lined with bitumen and pitch. And although the daughter of Pharaoh knew nothing about the God of the Jews, she, too, became the prism of God's divine providence when she found the child and rescued him from exposure. She who knew not the compassionate God through faith enabled the compassion of God to be revealed through the prism of her compassion, that others might discern, with faith, the presence of God.

Somewhere I read, "To search for Christ is to find him." The searching is the finding, and as we search to find him in our history, the Holy Spirit widens within us the capacity to receive God through faith. When we long for companionship with the poor, the lordship of Christ longs for companionship with us. In the long run, that's the purpose of prayer.

QUESTIONS FOR YOUR REFLECTION

1. Has it been true in your life that, as you fixed your eyes on the poor, you found yourself fixing your eyes more intently on Jesus?

2. Why is prayer absolutely essential as we fix our eyes more and more on the poor?

3. Can you recall historical circumstances in your own life that God used to direct and form your life?

4. In what way is the remembering of the historical events of your own past life a splendid way of praying?

SATURDAY AFTER ASH WEDNESDAY

We Are Sacraments of God's "I Am"

WORD

"Moses said to God, 'When I go to the Israelites and. . . they ask me, "What is his name?" what am I to tell them?' God replied, 'This is what you shall tell the Israelites: "I AM" sent me to you'" (Exod 3:13-14).

REFLECTION

Our relationship with God is paradoxical. The more others demand that we serve them the less free we become. But with God, it is the opposite. The more God calls us to service the more free we become. Service to God is friendship with God. Jesus said to his disciples: "I do not call you servants any longer, for a servant does not know what his master is doing. Instead, I call you friends, since I have made known to you everything that I have learned from my Father" (John 15:15).

Why is service to God friendship with God? Because God is love. It is the nature of God to fill us with the goodness of God. God, like the light of fire, envelops all of creation. God is wholeness, and in that wholeness is God's holiness. God chose to be identified as "I Am." God's creation groans, waiting to be filled with the liberating presence of an I Am-ness that gives it purpose. God's I Am makes all of reality holy. God is not an object to be inspected but a wholeness to be experienced and enjoyed. How, for example, can I stand in sunlight and define for those in darkness what light is? If the light could speak, it could only say, "I am light!"

What is God's I Am? On one occasion a teacher asked a class of high-school students, "If you had the power to make God cease to be God, what would you remove?" One of the students responded, "I would remove God's longing to be with others." Did the young man realize that what he would remove from God is the name Isaiah gave to God, "Emmanuel," which means "God is with us"?

God's withness is God's I Am-ness. Notice again what God said to Moses: "I AM sent me to you" (see "Word" above). Examine the implications! In the act of creation, God endowed human nature with that same I Am-ness which is God's I Am. We are created in the image and likeness of God, and we bear God's I Am propensity to be sent and to be with. This is how we are the image and likeness of God. This withness, this solidarity with God and others, demands that we serve God by being with others in their needs, to be I Am for others. It is in serving others that we become sacraments of God's I Am and of God's longing to be with us. The I Am-ness of God has made the whole universe holy ground, and our willingness to serve others enables them to experience the holiness of God through our mediation. This is why we are a priestly people.

Our service to God adds nothing to God, but it liberates us to become all that God created us to be. This is the meaning of freedom. God is freedom because God is I Am. God's I Am is an infinite longing to be with us, to serve us, and to fill us with blessings. Our salvation, then, is to follow this way of God that was marked out for us by Jesus, who "though he was in the form of God, . . . did not deem equality with God something to be grasped at" (Phil 2:6).

The mind is boggled! The Son of God externally surrenders his triune withness that he might be God's I Am with all men and women. Service to others, then, is the way we empty ourselves, and it is this service that becomes our salvation because it is our freedom to share the I Am of God with others. It is a surrender that turns out to be salvation and a servitude that turns out to be freedom.

QUESTIONS FOR YOUR REFLECTION

1. What is the connection between God's name, "I Am," and Isaiah's name for the virgin-born, "Emmanuel," that is, "God is with us" (Isa 7:14)? In other words, if God is I Am, must he be with us?

2. If you remember the *Baltimore Catechism,* you will recall that God created us so that we might know, love, serve, and be happy with God for all eternity. Might it also be true that God created us that God might know us, love us, serve us, and be happy with us for all eternity?

3. Why is service done for God and others liberating? What is the difference between obedience and subservience?

4. When are you most free and happy, when you have all you want to have and do all you want to do or when you are free to become all that God longs for you to become?

From the Ends of the Earth

WORD

"What single individual can cry from the ends of the earth? The one who cries from the ends of the earth is none other than the Son's inheritance. . . . This possession of Christ, this inheritance of Christ, this body of Christ, this one Church of Christ, this unity that we are, cries from the ends of the earth" (St. Augustine, bishop).[3]

REFLECTION

Christ never cries out to the Father alone. We are the embodied, ecclesial presence of the risen Christ. As members of the Church, we enable Christ to cry out "from the ends of the earth." How powerful is the catholicity of this ecclesial kingdom of Christ on earth as it is in heaven! How powerful our communion with the risen Christ living his humanity today through the Church, with the Church, and in the Church! We are made one by the very life of Jesus, whose Spirit dwells within us making us one with God and with one another. This communion of our humanity with God's Word becomes the powerful voice of Christ's Word before the Father. God is moved because the Word is his own beloved Son, embodied with our belonging, voicing our pleas to the Father from the ends of the earth.

When each of us suffers temptation and we cry out to the Father, it is Christ who cries out to the Father. He whose humanity suffered all that Satan could hurl at him knows the depths of our trials. The Father hears our prayers because the Father always listens to the prayer of the Son. By means of the incarnation, Christ graced all of humanity to be one with him as he is one with the Father. When Christ was tempted by Satan, all of humanity was tempted. When Christ overcame the temptations of Satan, all of humanity overcame the temptations of Satan. When Christ cries out to the Father, "from the ends of the earth," all the ends of the earth cry out to the Father.

This powerful truth undergirds the meaning of worship. When we gather to celebrate the Eucharist, we gather not as individuals calling upon God to hear individual pleas in an atmosphere of togetherness. We gather as the body of Christ, a body whose communion with Christ and one another enables that corporate voice of Christ to call out to the Father from all the ends of the earth. This is the meaning of worship! The Father hears this ecclesial plea not because it is from a huge worldwide organization of individuals but because it is the body of Christ, the Church.

God heard Moses not because he was one individual pleading with God to liberate the chosen people. God heard Moses because he spoke in the name of God's people. But God heard the Son of God not only because he spoke as the Son of Man but also because he spoke as the Son of God. These credentials make our temptations and our trials open to redemption. Because of Christ as Son of Man and Son of God, our temptations and trials have worth in the sight of God. St. Augustine writes: "Our pilgrimage on earth cannot be exempt from trial. We progress by means of trial. No one knows himself except through trial, or receives a crown except after victory, or strives except against an enemy or temptations."[4]

Lent calls us to re-own our dignity—our worth—as members of Christ's Church, his body. To be redeemed is to be re-owned. Nothing is powerful enough to keep us estranged from God except the illusion that each of us can go it alone. The Fathers of the Second Vatican Council write:

> Just as God did not create men to live as individuals but to come together in the formation of social unity, so he "willed to make men holy and save them, not as individuals without any bond or link between them, but rather to make them into a people who might acknowledge him and serve him in holiness" (The Documents of Vatican II)[5]

The bond, or link, among all men and women is Jesus Christ. God does not ignore our individuality. God cherishes it! It is this very individuality, so unique and distinct in each of us, that enables the presence of the risen Christ to assemble the ecclesial communion that arises from the diversity of individuals. This communion, in union with Christ, is called the Church. Precisely because this body of people is sealed with the presence of Christ can it invite our trust. And because the presence of the risen Christ here upon earth bears the identity of our humanity can Christ cry out with one voice from the ends of the earth.

QUESTIONS FOR YOUR REFLECTION

1. When you pray, do you think of yourself as a significant and integral part of Christ's prayer before the Father? Or do you often feel as if your cry to the Father is just one of millions clamoring for God's attention?

2. What is the difference between the Church as organization and the Church as organism? Which of the two do you think has received the most emphasis in your lifetime? Do you think that the difficulties people have with prayer today are connected with their overall concept of Church, for example, Church as organization or Church as organism?

3. In the light of this chapter's reflection, how would you respond to those who say, "I don't go to Mass anymore because I don't get anything out of it"? Does this type of question come from people who view Church as "organization" or Church as "organism"?

Contracts? Not God's Way of Being Fair!

WORD

> "God said to Moses, 'I . . . established my covenant with them, to give them the land of Canaan, the land in which they were living as aliens'" (Exod 6:2-4).

> "[God] has given abundantly to all the basic needs of life, not as a private possession, not restricted by law, not divided by boundaries, but common to all, amply and in rich measure" (St. Gregory Nazianzen, bishop).[6]

REFLECTION

When the Fathers of the Second Vatican Council revived the concept of "the people of God," they drew upon an ancient biblical tradition. The implications of this title are enormous. To be God's people is literally to be owned by God and to share in the astounding generosity that accompanies that ownership.

When we begin the Nicene Creed at the Sunday liturgy, we recite the words, "We believe in one God." This expression of faith is much more than an intellectual assent to God's existence. It carries with it a corresponding belief that the God to whom we give our assent is the God who by covenant has consented to be faithful to a people God cherishes and calls God's very own. This consent is unconditional! It is a consent which bears absolutely no likeness to the contractual conditions we sometimes set up as criteria for our dealings with others. Recall the parable we often find difficult to understand. It tells of four groups of laborers hired at various times during the day. The group hired at the end of the day is paid the same wages as those hired at the beginning of the day (see Matt 20:1-16).

As we listen to this Gospel story we tend to question the unfairness we see suggested in the parable. Why? Because we are listening to the parable with contractual ears. Jesus doesn't deal with us contractually. God relates to us by way of covenant. There are no conditions in God's covenanted promises other than the astounding generosity and fidelity we regard as outrageously unfair and exaggerated. To believe in God is to believe that God wants nothing more from us than grateful response to a love that staggers our understanding of love. God wants to be God, free to love as God loves. Love by contract is not God's way of loving!

While God relates to us by way of covenant, our response to God is all too often by way of contract. This is the point Jesus made when he told the story of the Pharisee and the publican (see Luke 18:10-14). For the Pharisee, salvation was contractual. Head unbowed, he declared that he was not like the rest of people, "grasping, crooked, adulterous," or what seemed infinitely worse, "like this tax collector." He fasted twice a week and paid tithes on all he possessed. "Look Lord," he seemed to say, "I kept my part of the contract. You owe me salvation!"

No doubt the Pharisee was a good man. No doubt the tax collector was a scoundrel. This is not Jesus' point. The point is, good or bad, both the Pharisee and the publican belonged to God as sons. Kinship with God wins salvation, and all men and women are sons and daughters of God. The creator wants nothing in exchange for divine love other than our hunger and thirst for repentance and the gift of mercy, that we might become what God had in mind right from the beginning—the image and likeness of God.

Our response to God's covenantal promises is the generosity we display with the gifts God has given us. We are related to one another by the grace that relates us to God. If we are God's people, then we are in the truest sense brothers and sisters of one another. We are bound to each other not by contract but by covenant. God "has given abundantly to all the basic needs of life, not as a private possession, not restricted by law, not divided by boundaries, but as common to all, amply and in rich measure" (see "Word" above).

QUESTIONS FOR YOUR REFLECTION

1. What is the basis of relationships between employers and employees as compared with the basis of relationships among husband, wife, and children?

2. Does legal title to private property entitle one to own and possess as much of this world's goods as one possibly can without the responsibility of sharing possessions with the poor?

3. Take another look at the quotation from St. Gregory Nazianzen in the reflection. "Common to all" is the basis of stewardship. What is the difference between "common to all," stewardship, and "common to all" Marxist Communism?

4. What do you think is the difference between contract and covenant?

5. Might "Lenten conversion" mean a shift from a spirituality that understands religion as contract to one that understands religion as covenant?

A Success You Can Take with You

WORD

*"The LORD spoke to Moses, [saying] 'I am the LORD. Re-
peat to Pharaoh, King of Egypt, all that I tell you.' But Moses
protested to the LORD, 'Since I am a poor speaker, how can
it be that Pharaoh will listen to me?'*

*"The LORD answered him, 'See! I have made you as God
to Pharaoh'"* (Exod 6:28–7:1).

REFLECTION

I find nowhere in Scripture where God commands us to be successful. But written across the pages of Scripture is the invitation to be faithful
to the Word of God. God's work is the revelation of divine presence.
Ours is the instrumental role in that revelation. God begins that work
in us, and God brings it to a successful conclusion.

Those who seriously undertake to follow the Word must also take
seriously the imperative to obey the Word. Obedience is not a popular
word in a democratic society where freedom is associated more with
worldly success than with faithfulness to the Word of God. There is,
of course, nothing wrong with being successful in this world. Such success, however, is not freedom's goal. We are free when we can become
who God created us to be. We are not necessarily free when we possess everything of this world *we* deem necessary to be happy and
human.

Our problem with obedience is probably tied in with a prior difficulty with authority—how we define authority will determine how we
perceive obedience. Authentic authority peers past task and into mystery. Authority's power lies in its capacity to discern and to bring to
light the hidden giftedness and charisms of others. Authority is an exercise of love. What is uppermost to authority is not the task to be done
but the person to be discovered.

People are delighted and exhilarated when they are made aware
of their hidden talents, gifts, and skills. There is no better way for authority to attract people's listening than to apprise them of what is authorita-

tively seen in the mystery of their lives. This listening is called "obedience." It is the listening—the opening up—of one's fullest self, an activity so engaging that there springs forth the inclination to respond to the full person authority calls forth.

Authoritarianism, however, is preoccupied with power and task. It looks at persons as objects in terms of the skills they possess for the sake of its own narrow pursuits of power. Authoritarians speak often of obedience, but what they mean is subservience. Authoritarians care little for personhood's listening. They expect a response whose only aim is profit. Dogs and mules do as much.

God is the ideal authority because God loves persons. Dealing with Moses, God called Moses in a way Moses found difficult to accept because he could not see beyond what he perceived to be his failure in life, his speech impairment. God really needed this poverty of Moses in order to reveal strengths Moses was unaware of.

Who among us is not impaired? That doesn't mean that we are failures! Our impairments are truly our glory, for as St. Paul writes, it is in our weaknesses that we become strong (see Heb 11:34). No one can expect to be successful as architects of God's work here on earth. God calls us to only one success: that we faithfully listen to the Word of God, celebrate it, and let the Lord bear witness to God's holy presence here upon earth. It is through the power and the presence of the Word that *God* achieves success. It is this Word to which we respond that gifts us with the power of God's presence. "See!" God said to Moses, "I have made you as God to Pharaoh" (see "Word" above).

Now, that's a success you can take with you as you journey beyond the boundaries of a success you can't take with you.

QUESTIONS FOR YOUR REFLECTION

1. What is the difference between obedience and subservience?

2. How is obedience an exercise of freedom?

3. Recall at least one person who made you aware of a hidden strength and who challenged you to surface it and make it a part of your realized humanity. How did that person love you?

4. Do you see a connection between poor self-esteem and the success syndrome marketed by the media?

Jesus Christ Makes the Difference

WORD

"*[God] established a law for Adam, that he could not eat of the tree of life. He gave to Noah the sign of the rainbow in the clouds. He then gave Abraham, chosen for his faith, the mark and seal of circumcision for his descendants. Moses was given the Passover lamb, the propitiation for the people. . . .*

"*Jesus, our Savior, renews the circumcision of the heart for the nations who have believed in him and are washed by baptism: circumcision by 'the sword of his word, sharper than a two-edged sword [Heb 4:12]'*" (Aphraates, bishop).[7]

REFLECTION

It is not enough for the sophisticated rich to claim glory solely from the volume of their possessions. To be authentically rich means to be distinctively rich. A rich man of distinction will not be content with a large number of paintings. He wants as many as possible to be originals. That's what the distinctively rich mean by "going first class."

Aside from riches, our search for authentic identity reveals a hunger for distinctiveness. We choose to possess authenticity of personhood because we instinctively realize that we are different and unique. This drive within us is God-given. It was not by accident that God wanted to make a clear distinction between the Israelites and the Egyptians. God chose the Israelites to be distinctively the people of God and to bear in their identity the likeness of God. God did not create them to be like anything else in creation. What people adore is what people become. God created them to be like God.

God sent the image of God to become the image of humanity so that humanity might become the image of God. Jesus was the new Israel, who came as God's final covenant. Long before Jesus was born, God renewed again and again a tender intimacy with humankind by a series of covenants, each of them calling for distinctive responses.

29

These covenants were such that all peoples might know that the Israelites were the chosen people of God.

Jesus represented the final covenant God made with humankind. The sign of this covenant bore no mark of earthly distinctiveness—no tree of good and evil, no rainbow, no circumcision, no Passover lamb. The mark of the new covenant was Jesus Christ and his new way of living, distinguishing God's chosen people from all others. Christ's way of living was a new kind of circumcision, marked on the hearts of Christ's followers by "the two-edged sword of God's Word" (see Heb 4:12). God designed that a divinely chosen people should be distinguished from all others by the kind of love Jesus generously displayed.

We are authentic followers of Jesus not because we bear external, changing marks of distinctiveness but because we live by an unchanging covenant that gives meaning to the externals. Christian identity is marked not by a knife but by the waters of baptism. In that sacred rite, a former way of living marked by the spirit of this world is put to death. From these waters, God's new Israel emerges to live a new way, marked out by Jesus in the kingdom he came to proclaim here on earth.

Who, then, is the authentic follower of Jesus? What is the "true religion"? Surely we dare not revert to former times when religious identity was oftentimes measured by human marks of distinctiveness. Eating fish on Friday symbolized Catholic assent to the sufferings of Christ. Did it, of itself, guarantee a Catholic consent to live the way of life marked out by Christ's cross? Not really.

More to the point, the true followers of Christ, claiming membership in the "true religion," are those whose communion is marked by the values, the attitudes, and the priorities of Jesus. The people of true faith are those who, by their surrender to the Holy Spirit, guarantee that the two-edged sword of God's Word will carve into their hearts the identity of Jesus' personhood. That carving implies the pain of breaking with the spirit of this world. But if that is the sacrifice we are willing to share with Christ, his identity will become visible in a Church clearly distinguishable by her consent to carry the cross. We may also expect the identity of Christ's resurrection.

Christ's identity makes a difference in ours.

QUESTIONS FOR YOUR REFLECTION

1. Something has meaning if it makes a difference in your life. What does Jesus Christ mean to you?

2. What do you think is distinctive about Christianity?

3. If authenticity comes from the consistency between what we assent to and what we consent to, how would you rate the authenticity of the Christianity people say they believe and the Christianity they actually live?

4. If you were accused of being a Christian, what would be the evidence your accusers would offer as proof of their allegations?

To Remember Is to Be Re-membered

WORD

"Keep, then, this custom of the unleavened bread. Since it was on this very day that I brought your ranks out of the land of Egypt, you must celebrate this day throughout your generations as a perpetual institution" (Exod 12:17).

REFLECTION

The Passover is a celebration of remembrance. Both Jews and Christians gather to remember that the Lord does not forget them. Throughout Lent, we Christians recall our sins and ask God to forgive us. At the same time, we recall that God has made a perpetual covenant with us. God has promised that God will never abandon us. On Holy Saturday night our joyful alleluias are really glad cries of remembrance: "God has not forgotten us!"

Indeed, God does not forget us. At the same time, God calls upon us not to forget God. To the Israelites he pleaded, "Keep, then, this custom of the unleavened bread. . . , you must celebrate this day throughout your generations as a perpetual institution" (see "Word" above). Moreover, at the Last Supper, Jesus said to his disciples, "Do this as a remembrance of me" (Luke 22:19).

Our remembrance of Christ's redemptive act of salvation is not of an event frozen in the past. Remembering is re-membering. When we gather for the Eucharist, we are also re-membered as sacraments of Christ's love. We remember that embodied in our humanity is the graced capacity to offer Christ's love to the world. We gather to encounter the ever-present paschal mystery. At the Eucharist, we remember that Christ is ready to relive his dying and rising in our dyings and risings. In his remembrance of our sufferings and dyings, he is ready to own them as he owned his suffering and dying. This readiness to own *our* sufferings so that we might again be owned by the Father is called "redemption." This is the paschal mystery for us, the body of Christ.

Remembering is not a leap of the mind backward over centuries of time. To remember Christ is to engage, here and now, the power of Christ's ongoing redemption for a people gathered to celebrate that ever-present mystery. When we gather at the Eucharist, it is as a people who gather to celebrate the joy of having already been found by Christ. He is still the good shepherd, who continues to make the Passover journey with his Church, searching out all who are lost, ready to share deeply in that lostness. That we lose the way and are found again and again is the reason we gather to remember Christ. It is in that remembering that we are gradually re-membered. It is in that re-membering that we embody Christ's gift of the wholeness we call Catholicity.

Remembrance is not a mental gymnastic. It is a commitment to devote ourselves to the vocation of paschal mystery, a vocation that keeps the Church alive. If the heart of the Church is the love of Christ, remembrance is the breath of the Holy Spirit inspiring the Church to love like Christ. Christ's way of loving is the life of the Church.

To remember Christ is to enter the vocation of dying to sin and being raised by the Father to new life. Each of us is raised from the death of sin. In that daily death and resurrection, Christ, too, makes real the redemptive power of his own dying and rising. When Christ said, "Do this as a remembrance of me," he invited all of us into the vocation of his dying and rising, yet to be fully completed in the Church. We celebrate this vocation of dying and rising in the Eucharist, where daily the Lamb of God is offered as the sacrament of humanity's transformation into the image and likeness of Christ. This re-membering is worth remembering.

QUESTIONS FOR YOUR REFLECTION

1. One of the meanings of "redemption" is "to re-own." Can you connect this meaning of redemption with the vocation of dying to sin

and rising to new life in Christ? In what way is sin a *dis*ownership? In what way is grace the guarantee of true ownership?

2. Do you see any connection between being "re-owned" by Christ and the act of remembrance that he called us to as an integral part of the Eucharist?

3. Keeping in mind Christ's words, "Do this as a remembrance of me," do you see more clearly the obligatory nature of Sunday worship? Are we obligated to gather so that we might recall only the historical event of the Last Supper? Or are we obligated to gather that we might be engaged by the power of this ever-present mystery of "re-ownment"?

4. Why is the Eucharist a perpetual remembrance of Christ's dying and rising?

FRIDAY OF THE FIRST WEEK

Forgiveness, a Journey into Mystery

WORD

> *"Who could listen to that wonderful prayer, so full of warmth, love, of unshakable serenity—'Father, forgive them'—and hesitate to embrace his enemies with overflowing love? Is any gentleness, any love, lacking in this prayer?"*
> (St. Aelred, abbot)[8]

REFLECTION

The reason it is difficult to forgive our enemies is that we tend to draw boundaries around our understanding of mercy. We will forgive, providing reparation has been made. Mercy, however, has no conditions. It is grounded in a justice whose equity is God's creative purpose. This purpose, namely that God created the human person in the image and likeness of God, is the basis of God's justice and the reason for God's mercy.

33

When Jesus forgave his enemies, his absolution issued forth from a mercy that has no boundaries, no conditions, no qualifications. In the eyes of Jesus, sinners stood justified before God not because they claimed equity by way of earthly reparations but because equity was already theirs by way of God's creation. No earthly reparation can ever qualify as complete satisfaction for sin because it simply is not commensurate with God's creative purpose. The only reparation God requires is that we accept his mercy. That is why Jesus' parable sent the sinful publican home justified rather than the self-righteous Pharisee who offered his good works as equity for salvation (see Luke 18:14).

We find forgiveness difficult because we often relate to others along the lines of contractual justice. "If you do this one more time, I will have no more to do with you." This is conditioned forgiveness. If one has been contractually forgiven, the contract is considered as breakable and the obligation to forgive nullified if a subsequent rupture of the relationship occurs. Relationships built on such justice are not perceived as permanent and are, thereby, subject to nullity. God does not forgive that way—thank God!

Biblical justice is by way of covenant. The relationships of covenanted justice are permanent and indissoluble. Why? Because they are consistent with the way God relates. God's relationship with us is permanent and unconditioned because we have been gifted with never-ending mystery and purpose. Marriage, for example, is such a relationship. When two people wed, they consent to a vocation of calling forth each other's hidden and undisclosed selves. What each calls forth becomes the communion of a new identity. Marriage is permanent and unbreakable because the mystery of every human being is inexhaustible. When two people wed, they unite not only what they know of each other, they also unite what they *don't* know of each other.

Likewise, forgiveness is a ringing affirmation of mystery, of each other's "moreness." When we forgive, we call forth not only the mystery of another but also the mystery of ourselves and the self-esteem that is bound to result from that discovery. If I refuse to forgive another, I slam shut the door to my own fullest identity waiting to be united with the identity my forgiveness can birth from the womb of the forgiven's mystery. When I am under the illusion I can no longer forgive, I close the door to a possibility of being like God. There is no limit to our forgiveness because God created us to leap the walls of wounded pride and self-righteousness and share the mystery of his holy companionship dwelling in the realms of each person's undisclosed mystery.

"Lord," Peter asked Jesus, "when my brother wrongs me how often must I forgive him? Seven times?" Jesus replied, "Not seven times; I say, seventy times seven times" (see Matt 18:21-22). Which is to say that there are no limits to forgiveness because there are no boundaries to the mystery of the human person. Each of us is always much more than our imperfections disclose. When we fail to pass over one another's imperfections, we become angels of death dealing out finality to the fullness of undisclosed personhood the Lamb of God came to liberate and raise up.

Easter is much more than a holiday. It celebrates an ever-present reality which the Holy Spirit endeavors to awaken during the holy season of Lent. Easter is the celebration of people who have become "eastered." This Passover includes a determination to be a forgiving and merciful people. Not only does forgiveness by an eastered people liberate others from the constrictions imposed by egocentricity, it also liberates *them* from the egocentricity that justifies unforgiveness. To forgive another from the stance of covenanted mercy rather than from the illusion of contractual justice is to forgive one's own egocentricity. To pass over from conditioned forgiveness to mercy's "seventy times seven times" forgiveness is the pain of Lent but the joy of Easter!

QUESTIONS FOR YOUR REFLECTION

1. A little boy gave this reply when asked to give the meaning of salvation: "Salvation," he explained, "is putting things back where they belong!" How does forgiveness fit in with his reply?

2. How is the sacrament of forgiveness and reconciliation a celebration of God's covenant with his people?

3. In the story of the prodigal son (see Luke 15:11-32), why are we sometimes inclined to sympathize with the elder son as he voices complaints to his father? What is the difference between how the father regards the repentant son and how the elder son regards his brother's return?

4. Can you recall a time when your unconditional forgiveness opened the door to another person's deepest identity?

Raising Questions Is the Answer

WORD

> *"The LORD said to Moses and Aaron, . . . 'If your son should ask you later on, "What does this mean?" you shall tell him . . .'"* (Exod 13:14).

> *"In the face of the way in which the world is developing today there is an ever increasing number of people who are asking the most fundamental questions or are seeing them with a keener awareness* ("The Church in the Modern World").[9]

REFLECTION

Faith is renewed and strengthened not because religion promises to provide answers to new questions raised by technology but because religion offers to shed light on questions that transcend the parameters of technology's expertise. It is well within the competency of technology to say, "Here is what it is." But the question, "What does it mean?" may need the light of faith.

Though faith leads us to light, it first invites us to pass through the darkness of our limitations. Before faith can take us to light, it helps us to live without fear while darkness prevails. Faith enables us to see that ultimate answers cannot be found, even in religion's disciplined dedication to liberate humankind from darkness. Religion that promises answers for every question becomes an ideology. One cannot calculate the harm done by religious extremists who offer as fundamental and ultimate shallow answers to questions that transcend ideology. The supreme delusion is in giving people the impression that religion with all the answers leads to salvation.

Faith thrives when questions abound. We are not without salvation simply because we don't have all the answers. When fundamental questions are raised, faith leads us beyond the boundaries of answers deemed by some to be ultimate. Faith assures us that, while we do not have earthly answers for eternal questions, there always remains the consolation that the one who offers our faith eternal questions also knows the earthly answers. Fundamentalism is not harmful because it addresses fundamentals. It is harmful when its foundation is its answers for questions that make faith unnecessary and irrelevant.

Likewise, technology is not an evil because it is technology. It becomes harmful when it identifies itself as the ultimate, complete, and final solution to all human questioning. It deludes when it offers itself as the perfection and totality of all human satisfaction. It becomes the ultimate delusion when it substitutes itself for faith.

The Church stands in the midst of people's lives not to provide solutions for problems technology has raised but to shed the light of faith on fundamental questions. These are the questions that transcend the boundaried solutions Adam and Eve chose as the replacement for their once-graced vision of reality. They were created in such a way as to have God at the center of their lives. At the serpent's suggestion, they chose as the ultimate answer a created good to be the center of their paradise.

Jesus is the center of our lives not because he came to bring all the right answers but because he came to invite us to a faith that sheds more than enough light on questions worth technology's attention. If, however, technology endeavors to portray itself as the ultimate answer and meaning of human existence, it will ultimately raise fundamental questions about itself. Fundamentalists might also reflect on this.

QUESTIONS FOR YOUR REFLECTION

1. If the purpose of religion is to provide all the answers to fundamental and ultimate questions, is there really any need for faith?

2. Why is the illusion that "religion is for answers" an invitation to pride? Why is that illusion dangerous to faith?

3. What are some of the questions to which you have been unable to find satisfactory answers? Is this a deterrent to your faith? Your hope?

4. Has your faith been strengthened despite your inability to grasp the mystery?

Transfiguration? But Climb the Mountain First

WORD

> *"The LORD preceded [the Israelites] in the daytime by means of a column of cloud to show them the way, and at night by means of a column of fire to give them light. Thus they could travel both day and night. Neither the column of cloud by day nor the column of fire by night ever left its place in front of the people"* (Exod 13:21-22).

REFLECTION

Faith does not call us to relate to God in a vacuum. While it invites us to hope for that which transcends earthly and human limitations, faith never depreciates or deprecates those limitations. When faith ignores human limitations, it runs the risk of being an ideal to be admired rather than a glory to be experienced. The existence of human limitations does not mean that their reality and the reality of faith are incompatible. When the gift of faith is fully alive, human limitations are at faith's service, groaning to be transfigured as servants of faith.

The Exodus of Israelites from Egypt was a monumental exercise of faith. Their faith, however, was not a guarantee against losing the way. The people needed human guidance not because they didn't trust God but because they needed to see where God was leading them across the desert. Faith in God is not weakened because one needs light for the darkness. One may have no problem whatsoever in believing that safety lies on the other side of the mountain. Faith in what's on the other side isn't the problem. Getting there is.

When God led the Israelites with a cloud by day and a pillar of fire by night, he addressed not their weak faith but their ignorance of the terrain. It is one thing to believe with the eyes of faith that God will lead; it is another thing to see with the eyes of the body where the person chosen to lead is going.

To be permitted to see with the eyes of the body what is to be believed with the eyes of faith is not an indictment against faith. For the

38

briefest time, Jesus allowed Peter, John, and James to see with the eyes of the body what God requires of the eyes of faith. This was not because their faith was weak but because their eyes enabled them to see that faith in Jesus' leadership was not unreasonable. So it is with us. Our bodily senses do not comprehend fully what faith invites us to, but we can apprehend the possibility that the call to faith is not unreasonable.

When Christ stood transfigured before the disciples, his was a transfigured humanity they beheld. What Christ offered them was the possibility of human transfiguration. Christ became human not to change humanity into something it was not created to become but to call it to the purpose for which it was created.

Instead of asking us to believe in God's existence as our first act of faith, God may be asking us to believe in the transfigured glory of our graced humanity. Faith may well begin not with faith in God but with faith in God's plans for our transfigured human personhood. To believe in human transformation is to accept our humanity as the incarnational habitat of faith. That is precisely the way Jesus of Nazareth dwelt on earth, and it is precisely the way the risen Christ dwells in the body of God's people.

The transfiguration was not so much God's invitation to Peter, John, and James to see with their eyes what heaven was like. It was God's invitation to see momentarily with their eyes what the kingdom of heaven on earth can be like for all who choose to believe in the transformation of humanity through faith. The transfiguration was not because Jesus was forced to give in to human limitations but because he wanted all of us to believe that faith in a humanity called to be transfigured with God's glory is not unreasonable.

QUESTIONS FOR YOUR REFLECTION

1. In light of the transfiguration story, why is the act of putting faith in one's human dignity a display of faithfulness in Jesus Christ?

2. Is it possible for a person with poor self-esteem to have a wholesome faith in God? Give a reason for your answer.

3. In what way does faith in God become unreasonable for people who do not love their humanity or put their faith in it?

4. In what sense is faith the transfiguration of our humanity? Can your faith be healthy if your attitude toward the human is unhealthy?

5. What does "incarnation" mean?

A Good Reason to "Keep Still"

WORD

"Pharaoh was already near when the Israelites looked up and saw that the Egyptians were on the march in pursuit of them. In great fright they cried out to the LORD. And they complained to Moses, 'Were there no burial places in Egypt that you had to bring us out here to die in the desert? Why did you do this to us? Why did you bring us out of Egypt? Did we not tell you this in Egypt, when we said, "Leave us alone. Let us serve the Egyptians"? . . .' But Moses answered the people, 'Fear not! Stand your ground, and you will see the victory the LORD will win for you today. These Egyptians whom you see today you will never see again. The LORD himself will fight for you; you have only to keep still'" (Exod 14:10-14).

REFLECTION

We find it difficult to handle freedom because our need for the security of possessing jeopardizes freedom's purpose. That security may guarantee the freedom to have; it does not guarantee the freedom to be. When the Israelites lived in Egypt, they were assured of food, shelter, and a place to be buried. They had everything slaves have. What they did not have was the opportunity to become more than slaves. They were free to have what was becoming to slaves. They were not free to be what was becoming to human dignity and human existence.

There are things we need to have. We need food, drink, clothing, shelter, and, yes, a place to be buried. There is not one of these things, however, that we can carry beyond the horizon of our last breath. But there is one possession we can take with us as we depart this life's temporalities—our human dignity. This is a possession whose worth extends beyond the temporality of having. It is a possession that gives us our reason to be. Being human is worth eternity because God created our humanness to be eternal. This divinely given possibility gives freedom its meaning.

There took place in the desert of the Israelite Exodus a confrontation between the freedom to have and the freedom to be. God's chosen people were ready to renounce the latter so that they could repossess the former. Possessing the freedom to have may have restored the security of having. But the Israelites forgot that having, acquired at the price of being, guarantees only slavery.

Does God need our haves to reveal divinity? Not at all! What God really wants from us are our have nots. How can the God who created from nothing be expected to reveal divine identity from the somethings we possess? Our ultimate beatitude is not in the things we have; it consists in God's fullness revealed in what we do not have. This is why Jesus began his preaching ministry by saying, "How blest are the poor in spirit: the reign of God is theirs" (Matt 5:3).

When the Israelites saw Pharaoh and his troops pursuing them, they were brought face to face with their poverty. They possessed absolutely nothing commensurate with the awesome earthly power of Pharaoh hard on their heels. Yet they possessed a poverty commensurate with God's sovereignty. Their nothingness matched God's allness. What God wanted from the Israelites was not the illusion of sovereignty that possessions can feign but the possession of the strength to be a divinely chosen people whose poverty attracts God's lordship and sovereignty. It is in this poverty God's identity is revealed.

Having this world's possessions is not an evil. The attitude that the goods of this world are worth our ultimate attention is. Adam and Eve fell for the lie that a created good would make them like God (see Gen 3:5). How ironic that they fell for the lie! They were already created in the image and likeness of God.

We are candidates for transfiguration not because we have what this world offers but because we have the capacity to become the image and likeness of God. We stand our ground not on this world's possessions and their passing delights but on our faith that God has called us to a journey toward a transfigured existence. This world is our Exodus experience. With God's gift of faith, we touch God's ultimate purpose for our human existence, even when its ultimate destiny, transfiguration, is not fully experienced in this world. Not to have the fullness of our transfigured identity is to live on earth poor in spirit.

For now it is enough to know that "the LORD himself will fight for you. You have only to keep still" (see "Word" above).

QUESTIONS FOR YOUR REFLECTION

1. How would you handle a statement like this: "For me freedom is the capacity to say what I want to say, do what I want to do, and have what I want to have"? If you agree with that statement, why? If you disagree with it, wherein lies its fallacy?

2. Why is security to have more enslaving than security to be?

3. What does "freedom to be" mean?

4. To what extent can "poor in spirit" be an indispensible condition for authentic freedom?

5. If the possessions of this world become the focus of one's total attention, in what way has one lost the most basic freedom? What is that most basic freedom?

The Good News of Good Friday

WORD

"How could God the Father ever cast off and abandon his only Son, who is indeed God with him? Yet Christ, nailing our weakness to the cross . . . cries out with the very voice of our humanity: 'My God, my God, why have you forsaken me? [Matt 27:46]' " (St. Augustine, bishop)[10]

REFLECTION

Alleluias are often mumbled because we refuse to let the death of Christ be good news. This is not to say that Christ was spared the agony of crucifixion. Rather, the joy of his death lies in the redemptive meaning of the crucifixion, a meaning that too often escapes us.

We allow the meaning of Christ's crucifixion to escape us because we refuse Jesus the fullest meaning of the death he chose not to escape. Like survivors who dress their beloved dead to look as if they were still alive, we mask the death of Jesus with the facade of our view of death so that we might mask ourselves with the facade of our view of life. We refuse Jesus the fullest meaning of death because we refuse to be as serious about the fullest meaning of life as we are about our view of death. The Scriptures unnerve us because their authors are far more honest than we about the extent to which Jesus died and, by implication, the extent to which we need to die.

An example of scriptural honesty about the death of Jesus are these brutally serious words of St. Paul: "For our sakes God made him who did not know sin to be sin, so that in him we might become the very holiness of God" (2 Cor 5:21). To be sin? St. Paul's honesty stuns us. "We don't want our Savior wallowing in our sinfulness" is the shallow response we make to a mystery of faith that promises unspeakable joy to those who permit Jesus to be made sin.

St. Paul's frankness is not an admission that Jesus became a sinner. Jesus was made sin because, as the new Adam, he exposed Adam's embrace of the serpent's claim: that God's created goods make human nature equal to God's uncreated nature. That's the lie! Jesus was made

43

sin so that his death might expose the sham that caused Adam's shame. The joy of Christ's death is not that he suffered a cruel death on the cross. The joy of Christ's death is humanity's restored claim to the glory of creaturehood's purpose: to be in the image and likeness of God. That creaturely purpose is humanity's hope of resurrection.

St. Augustine asks, "How could God the Father ever cast off and abandon his only Son, who is indeed one God with him?" (see "Word" above) What the Father cast off and abandoned was not the Son but the shame of the serpent's misrepresentation of the human nature God's Son embraced. Christ allowed himself to be made this misrepresentation so that the claim of the serpent's boast could be forever unmade, exposed, and thus rendered powerless.

St. Paul writes, "All of us who have been baptized into Christ were baptized into his death" (Rom 6:3). The death into which we are baptized makes way for our conversion. We proclaim the death of the Lord as often as we acknowledge and fully confess that the glory of humanity is not a lordship without God but a creaturehood bathed with the glory of God's lordship, graced to enjoy oneness and companionship with God.

Christ's exposé of the serpent's lie was unrepeatable. Our lives, however, remain exposed to repeatable lapses into hell's misrepresentations about humanity's purpose. Our hungers for God-likeness are oftentimes subject to futile fantasies, aimed at persuading us that the temporalities of this world can provide us with the sovereignty that God is. We are deluded when we believe these temporalities can assuage hungers for the eternal that only God's eternal sovereignty can satisfy. Christ was made sin? Shall we say instead, Christ was made the full implications of evil's lie that we might be made the full implications of Christ's truth? Once we die to the delusion of the serpent's claim as totally as Jesus died on the cross, we'll no longer mumble our alleluias.

QUESTIONS FOR YOUR REFLECTION

1. The first commandment reveals the source of all sin: "You shall not have strange gods before me." Recalling the above reflection, what do you think is the strangest god of all? In what way did Christ's death and resurrection expose it?

2. Why is it difficult for us to admit that Jesus was abandoned by the Father and that he died fully and completely as do all human be-

ings? What does this reluctance expose about our own attitudes toward creatures and the goods of creation?

3. After Jesus died, how did God's sovereignty reveal itself to Jesus? Why is this the alleluia we anticipate as we face our own deaths?

4. Recall one of Jesus' last words: "My God, my God, why have you forsaken me?" (Matt 27:46) When Jesus died on the cross, what precisely was the Father abandoning and calling all of us to abandon?

WEDNESDAY OF THE SECOND WEEK

"God Doesn't Answer My Prayers!" Really?

WORD

"As long as Moses kept his hands raised up, Israel had the better of the fight, but when he let his hands rest, Amalek had the better of the fight. Moses' hands, however, grew tired; so they put a rock in place for him to sit on. Meanwhile Aaron and Hur supported his hands, one on one side and one on the other, so that his hands remained steady till sunset. And Joshua mowed down Amalek and his people with the edge of the sword" (Exod 17:11-13).

REFLECTION

Pacifists may find the story of Amalek and the Israelites inappropriate. If the purpose of the story is to glorify war, the charge is justified. But if the purpose of the story is to symbolize the meaning of persistent prayer, then it is quite appropriate. The story is about the necessity of persevering in intercessory prayer as doggedly as the persistent Moses persevered with upraised arms.

But why persevere in prayer? Doesn't God already know our needs? Why is God silent while people pray persistently for needs God could grant in a matter of seconds? Why do people sometimes live their whole lives without seeing their prayers answered?

These are pertinent questions when prayer is perceived as upward chants for downward grants. Such questions about persevering prayer, however, may lose their pertinence when intercessory prayer is perceived as more than periodic notices to a heavenly welfare agency.

We persevere in prayer not to get God's attention. We persevere in prayer that God might get our attention. Prayer widens and deepens our capacity to embrace the "allness" of God. This allness compels the loving Lord to wait until our capacity to receive a fuller disclosure of God's allness is readied. God's waiting for our readiness is why we are asked to persevere in intercessory prayer. We persist in prayer so that we can gradually begin to understand that what we pray for is but a pittance compared to the fullness God is ready to unfold within the mystery of our lives.

God knows our needs far better than we! God waits. God will not grant us the "less" we imagine is worth our intercessions because God longs to flood our lives with the "more" human dignity is worth. God calls us to persevere in prayer for this earth's "less" that we might be graced to perceive heaven's "more."

The miracle of prayer, then, is not possessions God gives us but a transformation, awakening us to the realization that our possession of God puts us in touch with all possessions. Our persevering prayer enables the Spirit of God to enlarge our spirit's capacity for the fullest possible embrace of Jesus Christ and the kingdom he came to establish within us. To possess Christ as fully as our capacity permits is what holiness is. This is worth God's wait.

Meanwhile, we persevere in prayer so that we might be ready to embrace the allness of God, as we become more fully conscious of the totality of God's goodness. We persist, and we wait in that persistence lest we forget that God is humanity's allness.

Prayer is not what we are doing to God. Prayer is what God is doing to us, in us, through us, and with us. We do not pray as if to inform God of what we need. We pray persistently for lesser needs that the thirsts of our greater needs may be quenched. There is no need greater than to become like Jesus. This is the very purpose for which God created us. We pray for the lesser needs already known by God so that we may come to know the purpose of the human existence God calls us to embrace.

QUESTIONS FOR YOUR REFLECTION

1. Can you recall a gift from God that turned out to be far greater than the gift for which you were praying?

2. Did the greater gift in some way make a change in your relationship with God? If so, how would you describe the change?

3. In terms of needs not fulfilled as a result of your prayers, has there been a change in your desire to have those needs fulfilled? Describe it to yourself or to others.

4. If God always granted immediate fulfillment of every intercessory prayer, what do you think would be the nature of your relationship with God? Hint: what does "sugar daddy" mean?

THURSDAY OF THE SECOND WEEK

Responsibility: Care Shared

WORD

"Moses sat in judgment for the people, who waited about him from morning until evening.

" 'You are not acting wisely,' his father-in-law [said]. . . . 'you should also look among all the people for able and God-fearing men, trustworthy men who hate dishonest gain, and set them as officers over groups of thousands, of hundreds, of fifties, and of tens. Let these men render decisions for the people in all ordinary cases. More important cases they should refer to you. . . . Thus, your burden will be lightened, since they will bear it with you.'

"Moses followed the advice of his father-in-law and did all that he had suggested" (Exod 18:13, 17-22, 24).

REFLECTION

There is a variety of fears that deter us from the way to the Father. None is more detrimental than the fear of sharing one's leadership with others. When a leader assumes that his or her charism is *the* charism, *the* way for all, that leader indulges in buffoonery and will never be taken seriously except by means of the buffoon's exercise of coercion and tyranny.

True leadership is born of love and reveals love by calling forth the charisms of others. The charism of leadership inspires in others a sense of belonging rather than a sense of subserving. When people are assigned leadership roles, they, too, are expected to serve. Leaders serve best when they call forth not only the skills of persons but also personhood itself. In personhood's charisms dwell the instincts for belonging. Their fruits? Identity! This sense of belonging provides the integrity all institutions perceive as the ultimate logo for their identity.

The Church is not exempt from shared responsibility. No Church leader can fully express the way of Christ. "There are different gifts but the same Spirit; there are different ministries but the same Lord; there are different works but the same God who accomplishes all of them in everyone" (1 Cor 12:4-6). Love unifies this variety of gifts, ministries, and works, enabling the Church to become a sacrament of people's union with God and oneness with one another (see also the Dogmatic Constitution on the Church).[11]

The Church is well served not when leadership demands its way but when her leaders invite all the members of Christ's body to share the light of their giftedness, as together, in Christ, they journey to the Father. The Church is incomplete not because she is without the fullness of Christ's presence but because her membership has yet to grow more fully aware of Christ's presence. For this, the Church must wait until she is able to fill up "what is lacking in the sufferings of Christ for the sake of his body, the Church" (Col 1:24).

Moses acted wisely because he abandoned his fear that the Lord might not approve any but Moses' way of serving the people. He turned his former fear into the fear of the Lord that springs from love. He shared his leadership of the people so that the leadership gifts of others might give evidence of God's fuller leadership among all the people. No one member of a community can fully represent or reflect God's leadership until he or she can claim that a sense of belonging is developing in the whole community. Unless all the members of the body share their leadership charisms as members of Christ's body, disfigurement will mar the body's identity. When the claim of a Church leader is "Going My Way," the Church runs the risk of being little more than a back alley marked "dead end."

48

QUESTIONS FOR YOUR REFLECTION

1. Before the Second Vatican Council, priests celebrated the Eucharist with their backs to the people. Today, priests face the people as they preside at the Eucharist. What perspective is represented by each of these two methods of celebrating the eucharistic liturgy?

2. What are some of the many other ways the Church demonstrates shared responsibility today?

3. St. Augustine writes: "Become what you celebrate!" In the light of changed perspectives about Church leadership today, what do these words of St. Augustine mean?

4. Sometimes one hears the complaint: "If only Church leadership would tell us what to do!" What attitude does this reveal about those making the complaint? Is shared responsibility a sign of weakness among Church leaders? What is the strength that shared responsibility invokes?

FRIDAY OF THE SECOND WEEK

Israel, God's "Fair Lady"

WORD

"The LORD called to [Moses] and said, 'Thus shall you say to the house of Jacob; tell the Israelites: You have seen for yourselves how I have treated the Egyptians and how I bore you up on eagle wings and brought you here to myself. Therefore, if you hearken to my voice and keep my covenant, you shall be my special possession, dearer to me than all other people, though all the earth is mine. You shall be to me a kingdom of priests, a holy nation. That is what you must tell the Israelites.'. . . When [Moses] set before them all that the LORD had ordered him to tell them, the people all answered together, 'Everything the LORD has said we will do.' Then Moses brought back to the LORD the response of the people" (Exod 19:3-8).

REFLECTION

One would be hard pressed to find sacred Scriptures more nuptial than these: "You shall be my special possession, dearer to me than all other people" (see "Word" above). This marriage proposal of a loving God to the Israelites is an astonishing revelation of divinity's inner beauty. Think of it! God places complete trust in a desert tribe, choosing them to give witness to the mystery of God's own identity. "You shall be to me a kingdom of priests, a holy nation." God named the Israelites to be a people singularly chosen to unveil the mystery of divine faithfulness, intimacy, and tenderness.

Who is this "Fair Lady" God saw hidden in the raw and rough bearing of a desert tribe, this chosen people graced to be a mediating possibility for God's beauty? What indescribable loveliness moved God to pledge immovable, unshakable, and never-ending faithfulness to them and to us? Who are we that our beauty and our goodness provide God with endless possibilities for making holiness attractive, possible, and credible? What qualifies us to be the mediating instrument of God's ever-bonding covenant?

Is it really possible to answer these questions this side of eternal life? Not fully. But then, can husbands and wives clearly define the beauty that moved them to be permanently faithful to each other? If husbands and wives can see in the mystery of each other a beauty so endless that love can last even beyond death, might we not believe that God sees in us a beauty beyond our capacity to define? And what of the added nobility that obliges us (noblesse oblige) to believe that our humanity has been anointed with the waters of baptism to be a priestly people, enabling Christ to mediate the meaning of God's identity?

We stand before this mystery unable to describe the beautiful holiness of God. What is more, we don't even have an earthly word to describe the breathtaking beauty God sees in us, a beauty God is covenantly faithful to. We cry out with the author of Deuteronomy, "Who will go up in the sky to get it for us and tell us of it, . . . Who will cross the sea to get it for us and tell us of it that we may carry it out?" (30:12-13)

Formerly, God answered these questions for the Israelites in the desert with generous gifts of nature, like food and drink. In due time, earthly signs of God's love became inadequate, and God sent us the one and only Word perfectly adequate to describe the esteem God has for humanity. The Word is the Son of God, who became our food and drink. With our humanity, God priested us with that Word, enabling us to speak—to mediate—the beauty and holiness of God.

"Therefore, if you hearken to my voice and keep my covenant, you shall be my special possession, dearer to me than all other people, . . . You shall be to me a kingdom of priests, a holy nation" (see "Word" above). We show that we have heard God when this Word becomes our way of life. It is this way that mediates to others the incomprehensibility of God. Grafted on to the Word of God, our lives are able to "proclaim the greatness of the Lord" (Luke 1:46). It is by means of God's own Word that we are graced to respond in kind to the faithfulness of God's covenant. Because the Word has become *our* flesh, we can be faithful to God's Word, Jesus, the faithfulness of God. The Word qualifies us to become God's own special people, moving us to respond, "Everything the LORD has said, we will do" (see "Word" above). This is the response that moved Jesus to proclaim all of humanity to be God's "Fair Lady": "This is my body. . . . This is my blood" (Mark 14:22-24).

QUESTIONS FOR YOUR REFLECTION

1. As you ponder the above reflection, can you recall unlikely people whose lives moved you to some degree of conversion? Can you describe what it was about these people that aroused your admiration and awe, challenging you to make changes that enabled you to grow and mature?

2. Why does it frequently happen that God enables the most "unsuitable" people to be effective witnesses of his identity in the world? In this connection, what does St. Paul mean when he writes in several places that when we are the weakest we are the strongest?

3. Jesus became priest when he became human. What is the meaning of that statement? What astonishing implications does this hold for being human? In terms of service, what does the sacrament of baptism ordain that our humanity be for Christ in the world?

4. How is the story "My Fair Lady" a beautiful parable about the meaning of redemption?

"Send in the Clowns"

WORD

> " *'I, the LORD, am your God, who brought you out of the land of Egypt, that place of slavery. You shall not have other gods besides me'* " (Exod 20:2-3).

REFLECTION

Idolatry is both humorous and tragic. If we keep a sense of humor, our gods turn out to be clowns. If we are humorless, our gods become clones of ourselves. Idolatry is humorous when humility enables us to see the difference between the deities getting our worship and the deity we ought to worship. The humor is in the difference between what we think ultimate reality is and what it really is. When sanity prevails, so will humor. And best of all, conversion is "Oh yes! We'll also be able to enjoy the clowns."

Idolatry is tragic not because there is the bufoonery of deities competing for our worship. The tragedy runs much deeper. Idolatry touches on human identity. What we worship, we become. There's the tragedy! The earthly good to which we surrender our wholeness becomes the idol that transforms us into its image and likeness. We become its clones.

> Why should the pagans say
> "Where is their God?"
>
> Their idols are silver and gold,
> the handiwork of men.
>
> Their makers shall be like them,
> everyone that trusts in them (Ps 115:2, 4, 8).

In saner moments we may laugh at the ambiguity of our image making. Nevertheless, the ambiguity of an existence divinely designed for infinity but integrally bonded to finity turns out to be tragic when finity is preferred. That's the problem. From the womb to the tomb we must live in this world. We need its goods for survival, but we are puzzled when we read the advice of saints to take refuge from this world.

How does that advice square with Christ's own description of his Father's mission? "God did not send the Son into the world to condemn the world, but that the world might be saved through him" (John 3:17).

The ambiguity dissolves when we see that behind the apparent contradiction lies a dual understanding of world. There is world as spirit and world as place. The "spirit of the world" includes the attitude that the goods of this world are absolute, ultimate, and totally sufficient. The transcendence of having becomes the all-pervasive and exclusive substitute for the being God has called to transcendence. This well-defined spirit of the world bears the fruits of what St. Paul calls "the flesh." To the Galatians, he writes about the human identity flesh engenders: "What proceeds from the flesh [is this]: lewd conduct, impurity, licentiousness, idolatry, sorcery, hostilities, bickering, jealousy, outbursts of rage, selfish rivalries, dissentions, factions, envy, drunkenness, orgies, and the like" (5:19-21).

"Let us take refuge from this world" becomes, then, the prudent counsel of the saints. They perceive as tragedy the worldly spirit forming and shaping people into its image and likeness. Yet the world is a place where the goodness of God dwells. The world is good because God created it to be good. Dwelling within the finiteness of earthly goodness, the world will forever be "charged with the grandeur of God" (Gerard Manley Hopkins). [12]

The world is not evil because it is created. It becomes evil when the inhabitants decide that no other goodness lies beyond its createdness. Salvation is not defined by the temporalities of this world. Salvation begins when we restore the world to the dignity of creaturehood so that God's creatorship might liberate us from the caricature of playing God. Christ liberated us from the tragedy of an idolatry that makes us clones of the creation we have deified. And all the while, creation has never ceased groaning for someone to "Send in the Clowns."

QUESTIONS FOR YOUR REFLECTION

1. Since the very nature of a human being is to become like God, why is a wholehearted pursuit of having a dangerous way of living? Why is the pursuit of being a safeguard for salvation?

2. Created things (including human charisms and talents) are not bad because they are created. They become bad when they become ultimate. How would you explain and clarify that statement for the benefit of children?

3. The Church urges us to fast and give alms during Lent. How can these two Lenten exercises, faithfully kept year round, enable all of us to keep a balance between having and being? How do these exercises promote a good sense of humor?

4. Does "blest are the poor in spirit" refer to not having the goods of this world? Is it possible to be rich with the goods of this world but, at the same time, to be poor with the spirit of the world? If so, what's the key?

"If Only You Knew . . . !"

WORD

> "'A woman came' [John 4:7]. She is a symbol of the Church not yet made righteous but about to be made righteous. Righteousness follows from the conversation. She came in ignorance, she found Christ, and he enters into conversation with her. Let us see what it is about, let us see why a Samaritan woman came to draw water. . . .
>
> "We must then recognize ourselves in her words and in her person, and with her give our own thanks to God. She was a symbol, not the reality; she foreshadowed the reality, and the reality came to be. She found faith in Christ who was using her as a symbol to teach us what was to come. 'She came . . . to draw water.' She had simply come to draw water, in the normal way of man or woman" (St. Augustine, bishop).[13]

REFLECTION

It is impossible to recognize God's gift to us unless we first recognize the gift God wants from us—our poverty. Our wounds, hurts, failures, hungers, thirsts, and brokenness are the poverties that the Samaritan woman symbolized (see John 4:4-24). These are the gifts God

54

asks of us. What makes us right with God is not the fullness of our strengths but the strength of our weaknesses, which readies us to be filled with the gift of God's life.

The reason we do not recognize God's gift is that we do not recognize that poverty's strength is its giftedness to God. God's gift to us is to raise up Jesus from the crosses we freely share with Christ. Jesus died once on his cross, but he died in solidarity with all the crosses of humanity by which we fill up and complete Christ's own death. When Jesus was nailed to the cross, he linked divinity to humanity's poverty. His crucifixion committed him to our daily dyings. For that reason, he thirsts for us to invite him to share the gift of those dyings. It is this invitation that invites the Father to raise Jesus from the tombs of humanity's poverty.

Who are the poor? Surely poverty is more than the lack of physical needs. The poor are those whose human dignity has been violated. Such violence may even be self-inflicted. For example, the woman at the well hardly qualified as an expert on marital wholesomeness, a fact she was not able to hide from Christ's discernment. He did not gloss over her five marriages plus her live-in arrangement. Nevertheless, he did not repudiate her. He encountered her precisely at the point of her own self-inflicted brokenness, which, paradoxically, served as her claim to righteousness. She gave him her poverty when she confessed her sin.

God prefers the poor because poverty exposes injustice and leads us to ask, "What is the basis of justice?" This question moves the Father to make known to us that what justifies us and makes us righteous is God's purpose in creating us in the image and likeness of God. Here is the basis for human worth and worship. In the light of this worth, this justice, and this righteousness, whatever jeopardizes or enhances human dignity justifies God's attention. God blesses our strengths yet does not ignore the poverty of creaturely personhood that qualifies us for God's favor.

God's commandments rest on the foundation of human dignity, not on the human mastery of moral imperatives. Those who keep the commandments without addressing themselves to injustice provide garments for a self-righteousness that not only blinds them to injustice but also justifies injustice as evidence of the poor's failure to master the imperatives. Commandment keeping like this becomes little more than pious yea saying, which, Jesus warned, does not qualify for the kingdom of heaven (see Matt 7:21). And while egos may be well garmented with the self-righteousness of commandments memorized, recited, and kept, how blessed are those who appear before God's judgment clothed with the wedding garment of obedience to compassion for the poor, to whom Christ's commandments call us.

The woman came to draw water to slake the poverty of physical thirst. She revealed to Jesus in a shining moment of truth that another thirst burned deep in the mystery of her life. When she laid bare before Christ the magnitude of her deeper thirst, she gave to him the precise gift God needs to slake eternal thirsts. This precious gift of her poverty became the floodgate, opening up an ocean of living water to quench her thirst for eternal love. Her gift to Jesus, her poverty, symbolized the thirst God's divinity came to slake. Her poverty symbolized God's own indebtedness to humanity by way of humanity's purpose for existence—to be in the image and likeness of God.

QUESTIONS FOR YOUR REFLECTION

1. How did the scribes' and Pharisees' version of righteousness differ from Jesus' (see also parables like "the good Samaritan," "the prodigal son" and "the publican and the Pharisee")?

2. In the light of the above reflection, how would you go about drawing up a job resume for salvation, compared with the "job resume" described by the scribes and the Pharisees?

3. What is your "poverty"? Have you ever regarded it as a gift to God? Would that be easy? Is that what we mean when we say, "I'll offer it up"?

4. A person says to you: "This business of peace and justice is nothing but politics disguised as religion. My religion is to keep the commandments, no more, no less!" How would you respond?

"So What!"

WORD

"After Moses had gone up, a cloud covered the mountain. The glory of the LORD settled upon Mount Sinai. The cloud covered it for six days, and on the seventh day he called to Moses from the midst of the cloud. To the Israelites the glory of the LORD was seen as a consuming fire on the mountaintop. But Moses passed into the midst of the cloud as he went upon the mountain; and there he stayed for forty days and forty nights" (Exod 24:15-18).

REFLECTION

In his book *The Song of the Bird,* Anthony de Mello, S.J., tells the story of the salt doll:

A salt doll journeyed for thousands of miles over land, until it finally came to the sea.

It was fascinated by this strange moving mass, quite unlike anything it had ever seen before.

"Who are you?" said the doll to the sea.

The sea smilingly replied, "Come in and see."

So the doll waded into the sea. The further it walked into the sea the more it dissolved until there was only a very little of it left. Before that last bit dissolved, the doll exclaimed in wonder, "Now I know who I am!"[14]

Articles of creed and theological definitions guard orthodoxy of faith but are not necessarily the guarantee of a redeemed identity. "Who are you?" asked the salt doll. It was the wisdom of the ocean to answer not with doctrinal propositions about oceans but with an invitation to experience the identity of the ocean so that it could experience its own identity. So it was with Moses. God did not call him to memorize theological propositions about the deity. God invited him to experience the divine mystery within the darkness of an all-enveloping cloud.

Satan knows that diabolical tinkering with the truth of God's existence gets up-and-coming devils nowhere. When devils spread the word

57

that God doesn't exist, their hellish mendacity serves only to arouse interest in heaven's veracity. Far more bedeviling is Satan's subtlety that God's existence makes very little difference. That's classic deviltry.

One wonders if the most basic human instinct of earthly survival can survive the world's philosophy of having its temporalities. Take the lad whose suicide note read, "So what!" He may have cashed in his survival chips because he had become utterly bored with a life that taught him, "Live to get!" Ironically, he never got to live. He could boast of no more than his possessions, which, alas, turned him into their image and likeness. He dissolved into their temporality because he had heard no message calling him to dissolve into the limitless ocean of God's eternity. If a human being can not boast of possessing an identity attainable by the grace of faith, the most one can say of life is "So what!"

Belief in God is not just one of a number of ideals and values one files away for the day of reckoning. Even Satan believes in God. The boy whose last words on earth were "So what!" believed God existed. He no longer believed that God's existence made any difference to his.

When we say, "I believe in God," we are also saying something about human purpose and identity. To recite those words without the transforming implications their meaning holds is to relegate them to one's intellectual archives, where mental assent is more fitting than heart's consent. It is one thing to be convinced that God exists; it is quite another to be persuaded of the transforming possibilities of that existence. Conviction dwells in the mind, while persuasion inhabits the heart. When conviction weds persuasion, a human being moves toward the limitless ocean of God's creatorship, where human creaturehood finds purpose, meaning, and identity.

QUESTIONS FOR YOUR REFLECTION

1. If you did not believe that a personal, transcendent God existed, how would that disbelief alter the way you define yourself? With what would you define yourself? What would be the difference?

2. Why is having knowledge about God not necessarily a guarantee that God can be experienced?

3. Why are rules of morality, doctrines, and rituals (code, creed, and cult) necessary for the development of a healthy faith and an authentic identity? How does "knowledge about" safeguard "experience of"?

4. Does suicide necessarily imply that one denies the existence of God?

5. Integrity of faith demands assent to the existence of God and consent to experience that existence. What is the difference? Which of the two do you think is least understood and embraced by Christians today?

God Is Not a Reservoir

WORD

"Fasting is the soul of prayer, mercy is the lifeblood of fasting. Let no one try to separate them; they cannot be separated. If you have only one of them or not all together, you have nothing. So if you pray, fast; if you fast, show mercy; if you want your petition to be heard, hear the petition of others. If you do not close your ear to others you open God's ear to yourself" (St. Peter Chrysologus, bishop).[15]

REFLECTION

We need a new perspective for praying. Once upon a time we expected our prayers to move our reservoir-God to grant whatever we prayed for. One prayed for a job and expected to get either the job or some other comparable favor. Prayer, we imagined, was nothing more than tapping the God-reservoir.

Pray-ers today suspect that this is no longer the way it is. Our prayers don't seem adequate to secure from God solutions for the overpowering problems making their daily appearances on the evening news. One watches, for example, the hideous specter of hunger on the faces of countless numbers of Ethiopians and asks, "What in the name of heaven can my poor prayers do for them?" It's all so massive and overwhelming!

Starvation has always been massive. It isn't that there is more starvation today. Rather, the bad news of starvation has become more accessible, thanks to media technology. Our prayers seem inadequate not because we no longer believe in God but because the God we have imagined seems to have become an empty reservoir. Our God, as one author put it, has become too small. Is prayer, then, a waste of time? It is if we keep the inadequate perspective of the God-reservoir of our imagination. If we continue to expect our prayers to move God to do something about the problems we pray for, I think we are probably praying to a god whose reservoir has become a tomb.

I don't think that prayer's purpose is to get things done if it's God who is supposed to do all the doing. Prayer is not barter: "I will do the praying, God, if you will do the doing." The purpose of prayer is transformation of personhood. Prayer transforms our identities, so that we begin to see with the light of grace our own responsibility and our own part in the building of a better world. Faith is the capacity to see that God is more than a reservoir. Faith is the capacity to see beyond horizons that halt the eyes of our bodies. Faith is the capacity to see what God sees and as God sees. And what does God see? God sees a people created in his image and likeness.

Does this mean that we see the starvation of the Ethiopians as a new beauty and a new good? Of course not! Regardless of how one looks at starvation, it is always hideous. I mean that prayer works a transformation, whereby we begin to ask ourselves some very disturbing questions about what constitutes human dignity and human justice. Prayer raises questions about unjust and immoral economic and social conditions, which affluent nations may well be party to. Prayer causes us to ask the very questions God asks. Prayer other than God-is-reservoir prayer may not alleviate universal hunger this very day, but it may move us to ask, "Can I any longer accept as normative the fact that in one meal I eat more than the average Ethiopian eats all week?" Good heavens! What if millions of us started raising questions like that!

Effective prayer, then, will lead to fasting and the mercy of almsgiving. Why? Because both fasting and almsgiving provide an experience of conditions we pray God will attend to and correct. We fast and give alms that we might experience solidarity with the poor. Why is that important? Because Christ is in that solidarity. What God hears is not our prayers for the poor but the cries of the body of the risen Christ in solidarity with the poor. With fasting and almsgiving, our prayers become the cries of the poor who, in Christ, cry out to the Father. It is our identity with the poor and with Christ, with our hungers and deprivations, that brings about the transformation of the world from injustice to justice. We become the reservoir of goodness God invites us to minister.

Identity with the poor becomes the rationale for prayer. This does not mean that we cease praying for the poor. But our prayer needs to be accompanied by a sense of a felt personal responsibility for the problems that horrify us on the evening news. This sense of responsibility will begin to be resurrected in us as our fasting and almsgiving awaken the solidarity of want bonding us to the poor and to God. Christ has already told us where we can find him, and unless we walk with the least of his brothers and sisters, our prayers will draw from God about as much attention as an empty tomb.

QUESTIONS FOR YOUR REFLECTION

1. Recall an experience from your life that enabled you to identify with people who shared the same experience daily. What difference did this experience make in terms of your attitude toward these people? Could you say that this experience had a transforming effect on you? Describe it.

2. In what way could a successful regimen of strict fasting and generous almsgiving become a source of pride, resulting in even further estrangement of the poor from our lives?

3. If God always answered your prayers, what attitude between you and God would probably follow?

4. What is the connection between these two statements? "The purpose of prayer is transformation" and "Faith is the capacity to see what God sees and as God sees" (see "Reflection" above).

5. What does St. Peter Chrysologus mean when he writes, "If you have only one of them [prayer, fasting, and almsgiving] or not all together, you have nothing" (see "Word" above)?

Faith Scary? Comfortability's the Problem

WORD

*"Then Moses said [to the Lord], 'Do let me see your glory!'
He answered, 'I will make all my beauty pass before you,
and in your presence I will pronounce my name, "LORD";
I who show favors to whom I will, I who grant mercy to
whom I will. But my face you cannot see, for no man sees
me and still lives.'*

*"As Moses came down from Mount Sinai with the two
tablets in his hands, he did not know that the skin of his face
had become radiant while he conversed with the LORD"*
(Exod 33:18-20; 34:29).

REFLECTION

In a healthy relationship there are departure points. We must leave
zones of comfortability if we are to enter more deeply into the unique
mystery of another. This is as true in our relationship with God as it
is with human encounters. God constantly calls us into the mystery of
creatorship so that our own creaturehood may be nourished by the infinite bounty of divine moreness. Unless we are open to the possibility
of entering new realms of God's mystery, the health of that graced relationship may not be able to survive a familiarity that sets up zones of
comfortability, making God more pal than creator.

God calls us out of our zones of comfortability to encounter not only
divine mystery but also human mystery. We, too, have zones of mystery, untested and never before revealed or appropriated to our personhood. God calls us into the mystery of divine personhood that we
might encounter and appropriate the dimensions of human identity ly-
ing deep within us. We are like God not because we have the capacity
to become clones of God but because we have the capacity to relate
to the zones of God's mystery. In the mutuality of this human-divine
mystery, human personhood discovers hitherto hidden realms of self-
identity.

No relationship will ever last if those who commit themselves to another make little effort to seek out, explore, and call forth the other's unique mystery. The source of such effort is love, and it is kept alive and operative because true lovers are eager to see beyond their own zones of self-interest and human comfortability. This way of relating to those with whom we make commitments is a sign of the faith and love that assures permanency. Brides and grooms, for example, wed not only what they know about each other but also what they don't know about each other. If they are committed to the pursuit of the latter, their marriages will never die because there is no end to the mystery each pursues.

There is something scary about faith. Basically, faith is acceptance of God precisely at those junctures where God's moreness has never before been experienced. Faith is scary not because it calls us to make our assent to the existence of God but because it calls us to encounter that existence on unfamiliar terrain, where there are few comparisons to dissipate the scare. What is scary is not so much the prospect of encountering God but the prospect of encountering our own new identity.

We believe in God for more significant reasons than to give our mental assent to articles of faith. We believe in God so that the articles of faith and their implications, encountered at the point of mystery, will enable God to transform us and seal our beings with evidences of that transformation.

We are not called to peership with God. We are called to an identity of creaturehood in a relationship with God's creatorship. This encounter enables our humanity to radiate the holiness of God dwelling in the unexplored fullness of our own moreness. When that happens, it will probably occur to us that the eight Beatitudes are the radiance of God's face, shining in the lives of those who have been willing to impoverish themselves of the world's comforts. Unchanged images of God make zones of departure very difficult.

QUESTIONS FOR YOUR REFLECTION

1. Anytime there is an invitation from God to embrace a new image of the divine, it is a call to move on from a departure point. These departure points are our images of God. What is your image of God? Do you think your image of God has developed significantly?

2. Give examples of changed understandings you may now have of, let's say, democracy, marriage, friendship, parent-child relationships,

government, education, and so forth. If there has been a change in your images of these realities, did the change come about at the cost of comfortability with a previous image? If you were uncomfortable when you made the change, why?

3. When Jesus mingled with and ministered to the poor, the sinners, the lame, the blind and the deaf, and all those whose lives displayed abberations inconsistent with human and social norms of acceptability, the Jewish leaders were distraught with anger. What image of God had Jesus threatened? What image of God did Jesus proclaim? What was there about Jesus that was good news to the poor and bad news to religious leaders of his time? In our own time, is that good news or bad news for those who read the American bishops' pastorals on war and peace and the economy?

4. Why is it scary to leave one's zone of comfortability to move into the mystery of God? What does a move toward the moreness of God really involve?

Borne Aloft on Ego's Wings

WORD

> " 'Here, then,' said the LORD, [to Moses] 'is the covenant I will make. Before the eyes of all your people I will work such marvels as have never been wrought in any nation anywhere on earth, so that this people among whom you live may see how awe-inspiring are the deeds which I, the LORD, will do at your side. But you, on your part, must keep the commandments I am giving you today' " (Exod 34:10-11).

REFLECTION

Those who pray in spirit and truth are those for whom Jesus Christ has become the way, the truth, and the life. The prayer they offer arises out of a Christ-centrality. Like Mary, the sister of Martha and Lazarus, they have chosen the better portion (see Luke 10:41). This centrality of Jesus in the lives of Christians is called "discipleship." When disciples pray, they do so in the spirit of the truth, which is at the center of their human existence and, hence, of their identity.

At the heart of worship is the longing for Jesus to become both the centrality and the identity of human existence. Discipleship is a relationship wherein Christ has become central to one's human purpose. Doing good deeds is not the better portion of discipleship. The better portion is the wholeness with which we relate to Jesus Christ, the fruit of which is good works. "Any sound tree bears good fruit" (Matt 7:17). The process by which the centrality of Christ becomes real is called spirituality.

Spirituality is not a good feeling about deeds we have done for God. Nor is worship the shared good feelings of Christians who gather to be borne aloft on egos' wings. Worship is first the re-membering of people who gather to remember that Christ is the better portion of their humanity. This re-membering, this wholeness, gives discipleship an identity that transcends whatever stroking inflated egos require.

When disciples gather to worship, they are disposed to experience something more than good feelings about themselves. The spirit of God does not call disciples together to remember, recall, and recognize their human contributions to the betterment of the world. They are spirit-filled to remember and to celebrate the wonders of God, whose revelation transforms them to mirror the image and likeness of humanity's truest meaning, Jesus Christ.

Those who worship in spirit and truth gather regularly to sit at the feet of Christ and listen to his transforming Word. This presence of Jesus is the new covenant and the new law. To worship in spirit and truth is to sing "amen" to the centrality of truth itself, Jesus Christ. Discipleship means to have no other gods at the center of one's life. The law of the Christian life is Jesus Christ, and the centrality of his place in Christian living enables his prayer to become the prayer of all who pray.

The Word of God, Jesus, is God's law, which the Holy Spirit calls us to embody as Mary was called to em-body the Word: "The Word became flesh and made his dwelling among us" (John 1:14). The Holy Spirit is not calling us to adulate a historical figure named Jesus Christ at the safe distance of two thousand years. Jesus is the better portion of our lives now! His becoming flesh with our humanity and our sharing the divinity his presence heralds is called transformation. It is this transformation that re-members us as we celebrate the wonderful deeds God has done in us, through us, and with us.

Our Christened humanity moves the Father to answer our prayers. "Prayer," writes Tertullian, "is the one thing that can conquer God."[16] God is conquered not because we are uttering prayers but because, in our embodiment of Christ, God sees and loves in us what he sees and loves in Christ (see Preface VII for Sundays in Ordinary Time). God is conquered by prayer when Jesus stands at the center of human life as its better portion. This centrality enables us to worship in spirit and in truth.

QUESTIONS FOR YOUR REFLECTION

1. The New Testament reveals a tension between covenant spirituality and good works spirituality. How interesting that some of the New Testament characters with whom we oftentimes sympathize do not rank first place with Jesus: Martha, the elder brother of the prodigal son, the Pharisee in the parable of the publican and the Pharisee, and the vineyard laborers who worked all day but received no more than those who worked for only a few minutes. What do our feelings of sympathy for these people say about the kind of spirituality we practice?

2. We usually think of worship in terms of rituals and ceremonies. How does worship in spirit and truth widen and deepen the scope of worship? How would worship only as rite become a hindrance to a healthy relationship with God?

3. If good works are not the key that opens the portals of heaven, what, then, is their place in Christian spirituality? Is faith alone the key to Catholicism's "new theology"?

4. St. Matthew records Jesus as saying that at the last judgment the king will say, "As long as you did it for one of my least [ones] you did it for me" (25:40). Isn't this judgment according to good works? Upon closer look, however, can you discern covenant spirituality in these words of Jesus? What is the covenant implication of the word "least"?

Become What You Celebrate

WORD

"If the sacrament of the Lord's passion is to work its effect in us, we must imitate what we receive and proclaim to humankind what we revere. The cry of the Lord finds a hiding place in us if our lips fail to speak of this, though our lips believe in it. So that his cry may not lie concealed in us it remains for us all, each in his own measure, to make known to those around us the mystery of our new life in Christ" (St. Gregory the Great, pope).[17]

REFLECTION

Sacraments are not holy enticements to elicit Pavlovian responses to our nostalgic recollections of Christ's historical presence. Sacraments are ecclesial celebrations of the mysteries of Christ's risen presence and activity now, within the gathered presence of a people who make visible and real what they celebrate. Sacraments acknowledge a sacred reality that is both "already" and "not yet." The sacred reality is with us now in mystery; it remains yet to be while God's people journey to become the visible reality of the mystery they celebrate in the sacraments.

Christ lived on earth as the sacrament of his Father. His whole life was priestly because it was a continuous mediation of the Father. "Show us the Father," Phillip challenged Jesus. Jesus replied: "Whoever has seen me has seen the Father" (John 14:8-9). For Jesus, human life bore no meaning without its central relationship to the Father. Human life made absolutely no sense to him unless it mediated, revealed, and communicated the one reality forming and shaping all other realities.

What does this mean? It means that knowing the Father is what eternal life really is. It means experiencing God in a specific, unique, and radical way. This way reveals characteristics greatly at variance with patterns of living configured around the spirit of this world. To live as a sacrament of Christ in the same way Christ lived as the sacrament of his Father requires a radically different configuring center in our lives. With Christ as the sacrament of sacraments, we are called to offer our lives as a new "magnetic field," whereby all of reality is drawn to and arranged around Jesus Christ. "Indeed, the whole created world eagerly awaits the revelation of the [children] of God" (Rom 8:19). Our hope is this: that all of reality will bear the indelible seal of Christ's personhood. This is the reality begun in baptism and celebrated in all of the sacraments.

"If the sacrament of the Lord's passion is to work its effect in us, we must imitate what we receive and proclaim to humankind what we revere" (see "Word" above). Isn't this what discipleship means? Disciples are followers of Christ, in whom there is realized a consistency between what is ritualized at liturgy and what is made real in the marketplace. When a person is baptized, that person is sealed with the character of Jesus. The sacrament of baptism sounds a cry that pleads, "Do not let my cry find a hiding place in you" (see Job 16:18). Sealed with the character of Jesus, our lives are authorized to mediate the unmistakable characteristics of Jesus. These characteristics witness the way Christ's followers live and comport themselves. Christians are not disciples because they have learned about Jesus. They are disciples because they are becoming in their daily lives what the sacraments proclaim is already the reality. They are a priestly people because their lives reveal and make real who Jesus is. The Church can also say: "Whoever has seen me has seen Christ."

The Church is the sacrament of Jesus, and her sacraments are the actions of Jesus, which Church members are invited to mediate, represent, and celebrate in the name of Jesus *now*. From the cross, Jesus cried out, "Father, forgive them, they do not know what they are doing" (Luke 23:34). Who continues this cry of forgiveness today? Is it not those who have been commissioned by baptism to voice the cry of forgiveness Jesus uttered from the cross?

Those who have been baptized are challenged to become the living voice of that sacrament when they raise their voices to plead for murderers, adulterers, terrorists, rapists, thieves, liars, drug pushers, and, yes, abortionists. The reconciling voice of Christ raised in the Church cries out in behalf of these sinners, "Father, forgive them, they do not know what they are doing."

There are other cries of Christ too. The voice of Christ cries out through the hungry, the thirsty, the handicapped, the sick, the naked, the homeless, the bankrupt, the divorced, the children of the divorced, the elderly, the raped, and all who no longer feel a belonging that offers peace and joy.

Baptism calls us to be ministers of the cries of Christ, that is, stewards of the mysteries of Christ (1 Cor 4:1). Our lives were not created to become burial grounds where the cries for justice, compassion, and mercy are entombed in our lack of solidarity with the poor. Sacraments are not sacred things to be received for our own personal salvation. They are signs of a transformation, whereby our ecclesial identity displays unmistakable evidence of solidarity with the poor. When we celebrate a sacrament, we celebrate that mind which is in Christ. "I assure you, as often as you did it for one of my least [ones], you did it for me" (Matt 25:40). As we celebrate each sacrament, we share the identity of Christ, whose image and likeness we have been created to become. In short, what has been for us the "not yet" becomes the "already."

QUESTIONS FOR YOUR REFLECTION

1. The reflection speaks of a sacred reality that is both "already" and "not yet." In order to understand more clearly what this means on a spiritual level, can you identify this duality as it exists in various circumstances of your life? For example, how is "already" and "not yet" found in a new job, a diploma or college degree, the birth of a child, a wedding, the ordination of a priest or the vows of a religious, the cure of a serious illness, the decision to lose some weight, and the like?

2. In the Holy Eucharist, we speak of the real presence of Christ under the appearances of bread and wine. How is this sacramental presence both "already" and "not yet"?

3. Sacraments presuppose a kind of magnetic field that envisions Christ as the center of reality, drawing all created realities around himself. If Christ were, indeed, the center of all reality, what would that reality look like? Can you think of people who displayed in their lives a consistency between the "already" and the "not yet"? What were these people like?

4. How would you explain the line, "Do not let my cry find a hiding place in you" (see Job 16:18)?

Believable Signs Mean Believable Identity

WORD

"Then the cloud covered the meeting tent, and the glory of the LORD filled the Dwelling" (Exod 40:34).

REFLECTION

Identity crises in the Church take place when that which signifies is no longer consistent with that which is signified.

Religion needs renewal not because religious people have become bad but because religious people display an inconsistency between their religious symbols and their lack of significance in people's daily lives. Catholic identity is not well served, for example, when parents who are anxious to have their children baptized are not anxious to rear them according to baptism's ecclesial significance. Ecclesial identity is not guaranteed by the mere performance of baptism's rituals. It is guaranteed by the evidence of baptism's character indelibly sealed on the lives of the baptized.

The Second Vatican Council opened windows revealing an identity crisis already in progress. That council never intended to de-Catholicize Catholics, even though some are convinced that this is what happened. The Second Vatican Council called us to examine the problem of inconsistency between the Church's expressions of significance and a Catholic, lived experience of that significance. Did the Church's understanding of her symbols adequately address the many signs of distress that a hurt world displayed through its symbols of violence, war, and revolution? That the Second Vatican Council happened at all is testimony that the Church's understanding of ecclesial symbols needed to be addressed. We who make up the Church were too often content with doing the rituals without letting their significance speak out in the lived experience of our times.

It has been alleged that the Second Vatican Council disregarded two thousand years of tradition. This is not true. The Council invited us to examine two thousand years of tradition to discern in what way the Church shares an identity with Christ's risen presence in this world and with his infinite capacity to minister to each era's signs of the times. "Know that I am with you always, until the end of the world!" (Matt 28:20)

The Second Vatican Council was confident that what first-century pagans discerned in the small Christian communities could also be discerned in today's world. "See those Christians!" the pagans exclaimed. "How they love one another!" What identified the early Christians was a powerful love radiating from an interior union with the risen Christ. What awakened the pagans' admiration for Christians was a new revelation of love, which they witnessed in a body of people bearing the identity of Jesus.

The Church has a bearing. Call it sacramentality. Because the Church is human as well as divine, she needs to express herself humanly by signs and symbols—rites. Christians believe that the risen Christ dwells in the Church as truly as the Israelites believed that the presence of God dwelt in the ark of the covenant. For them, the presence of God was revealed by a cloud during the day and by fire during the night. Clouds and fire, however, are not the ecclesial evidences of Christ's presence today. The evidences of Christ's identity, signified and celebrated by the Church's signs and symbols, are his mercy and compassion. The identity of Christ is seen in the Church when there is revealed a consistency between the symbols celebrating Christ's mercy and compassion and the actual presence of Christ's mercy and compassion revealed in the lives of those who celebrate the Church's rites. When there is such consistency, the Church's identity is clearly evident.

The sacraments are ecclesial invitations to celebrate the call to become holy. We become holy not through mere performance of sacred rites. We become holy because we celebrate by means of sacred rites a sacred identity, revealing that the Word of God is at the center of our lives. The Word of God, as it once became flesh in the humanity of Jesus, seeks to become flesh in the humanity of a holy people. There will never be a serious identity crisis among Christians when there is a consistency between the incarnation as it took place in the humanity of Christ and as it takes place both in the rites of the Church's sacraments and in the lived experience of these rites by God's people. When there is a consistency between believable rites and the believable identity these rites signify, God's people will give witness to God's presence and power.

QUESTIONS FOR YOUR REFLECTION

1. Evangelization happens when there is a consistency between the significance of the sacraments ritualized and our lived experience of that significance. What does this statement mean to you?

2. What accusation do we lay ourselves open to when we are content with doing the sacramental signs without the corresponding intention of living according to sacramental significance?

3. What, for example, is the significance of the sacrament of reconciliation? What does its sacramental rite require of us as we live our daily lives?

4. What is meant by this statement in the reflection? "We become holy not because we perform holy rites but because we celebrate by means of holy rites a holy identity, revealing that the Word of God is at the center of our lives."

FOURTH SUNDAY OF LENT

The Whole Truth and Nothing but the Whole Truth

WORD

"The LORD said to Moses, 'Take Aaron and his sons, together with the vestments, the anointing oil, the bullock for a sin offering, the two rams, and the basket of unleavened food. Then assemble the whole community at the entrance of the meeting tent'" (Lev 8:1-3).

REFLECTION

In John Godfrey Saxe's poem "The Blind Men and the Elephant," six blind men from Indostan endeavored to define an elephant by the part of the animal's anatomy each chose to touch. With no capacity to perceive the elephant's wholeness, each defined it by the part he touched. Alas, each man was partially right, but because they failed to accept one another's experiences, all of them were wholly wrong. Each man's touch was wholly true in terms of what he touched, but no man's touch was the whole truth. T'was a paradox!

The worst blindness is to define the whole of reality by how it appears through the prism of one's experience. When we define God, religion, and Church by our experience of each, insisting that everyone accept as the whole truth our partial experience of the whole, we sow the seeds of division.

The poem about the six blind men of Indostan concludes with all of them engaged in loud and long dispute. They quarreled not because they denied the existence of the elephant. They quarreled because they denied the experience of one another's perception of the elephant. They failed to see that, even though each was partly in the right, their failure to accept one another's partial perceptions made all of them wholly wrong.

The word "catholic" means "wholeness." Catholicity is healthy when genuine and sincere efforts are made to reverence and cherish experiences of truth that lie outside the parameters of our experience. We are truly catholic when we welcome the opportunity of recognizing one another's capacity to experience God. A faith community does not come into being when all have been assembled to adopt someone's personal perception of religion. This is cultism. People are called and gathered that the gifts of all might be welcomed, shared, and celebrated.

Christ was rejected by the Jews because his claims didn't match theirs. According to their thinking, Jesus could not have come from God because he worked on the Sabbath. His healing of the man born blind caused the Jews to conclude, "This man cannot be from God because he does not keep the sabbath" (John 9:16). For the Jews, the Law was the totality and the wholeness of God's will. Whatever existed outside the parameters of the Law missed the mark of righteousness and, hence, was sinful.

Jesus was sent into the world to be light. His is the light that illuminates the limitless reality that extends beyond the limits of our capacities to perceive and to understand. It is not possible for any of us to understand the wholeness of God. We are, however, empowered with the light of faith to accept our incapacity to grasp God's wholeness and fullness. We may not be able at any one given time to have all the answers, but we do have the light of Christ to entertain questions yet to be raised. The real blindness of the six men of Indostan was each man's failure to ask, "Is there more to being an elephant that what I am touching?"

Lent's renewal calls us to let go of our glimpses of God for a faith vision that includes the moreness of God. To be ready to let go of our limited perceptions of God and to invite the light of Christ to shine more fully on our inward capacity to see the moreness of God's wholeness is at the heart of catholicity. When the whole community assembles at the entrance of God's fullness, its catholicity lies not in its understanding of God's fullness but in the truth that both God and kingdom of God are more than the assembly can understand. To accept that is to be also at the heart of Catholic faith.

QUESTIONS FOR YOUR REFLECTION

1. What is the difference between insisting that one's grain of truth is wholly true and that it is wholly *the* truth?

2. What is the difference between cult and religion?

3. Why is it impossible either on earth or in heaven to understand the wholeness and the fullness of God?

4. The word "catholic" is from the Greek *katholikos* meaning "toward wholeness." To what extent is this part of Catholic identity? At what point could Catholicism become denominationalism?

Atonement: Taking It Out on Christ?

WORD

> *"[Aaron] shall make atonement for the sanctuary because of all the sinful defilements and faults of the Israelites. He shall do the same for the meeting tent, which is set up among them in the midst of their uncleanness. No one else may be in the meeting tent from the time he enters the sanctuary to make atonement until he departs. When he has made atonement for himself and his household, as well as for the whole Israelite community, he shall come out to the altar before the LORD and make atonement for it also. Taking some of the bullock's and the goat's blood, he . . . shall render it clean and holy, purged of the defilements of the Israelites"* (Lev 16:16-19).

REFLECTION

The role of the Old Testament priesthood was to offer satisfaction to God for the sins of the people. The sacrifices that the high priest offered made up for transgressions against God and his Law. These sacrifices were regarded as a kind of equity whereby the people atoned for their sins and were made right, that is, made righteous or justified before the Lord.

One cannot help but notice a punitive tone in the Old Testament concept of atonement. Today's theological understanding of atonement does not portray an angry creator "taking it out" on the Son of God. It steers away from redemption as ransom, whereby Christ the high priest's death could be interpreted as an "eye for an eye" exchange for salvation. The death of Jesus is not regarded as a punitive assuaging of an infinitely offended God.

The death of Jesus on the cross was ample evidence of the barrenness of the serpent's claims to Adam and Eve in the garden. Hanging on the cross, Jesus literally called the serpent's bluff. Jesus hung on the cross as the Son of God who "did not deem equality with God some-

75

thing to be grasped at. Rather, he emptied himself and took the form of a slave, being born in the likeness of men" (Phil 2:6-7).

Jesus died not to assuage an avenging God but to give evidence that no earthly good can endow humanity with the sovereignty and lordship the serpent claimed it could. "The serpent said to the woman: 'You certainly will not die! No! God knows well that the moment you eat of it your eyes will be opened and you will be like gods who know what is good and what is bad' " (Gen 3:4-5). Jesus died on the cross to give evidence that our likeness to God is not by way of the possession of created goods. Our existence is justified by the gift of who we were created to be—children of God.

The very fact that Jesus became human is the revelation that humanity truly belongs to God and can never have meaning without that belonging. Jesus chose to die in a state of creaturehood so that God the creator might raise up all of humanity from its nakedness and barrenness to re-create, re-own, and restore it. The dying and rising of Christ, the paschal mystery, is the process by which we become one with God. This gift of belonging, by way of creation and grace, is our righteousness and our justice.

Christ's commitment to creaturehood without equality of sovereignty with God was the atonement Christ offered to the Father on our behalf. The very powerlessness and nakedness of Jesus, clear evidence that no created good could save him, was the "ransom," the justice, and the righteousness Christ offered to God and, now, we are graced to offer God.

Jesus died on the cross so that his Father might raise up all of humanity to be restored to oneness with God. By way of the cross, God wrested humanity away from the false claims of the serpent and restored it to its reason for existence. Stripped of the lies of lordship and endowed once again with the glory of creaturehood, all men and women became free through Christ's resurrection, to be again *at one* with the purpose of human creation: the image and likeness of God (see Gen 1:26).

QUESTIONS FOR YOUR REFLECTION

1. The serpent claimed that if the first man and woman would eat of the forbidden fruit they would become like gods. Why is this a lie?

2. In what way was the death of Jesus a repudiation of the serpent's claims? Why did Jesus yield his equality with God (see Phil 2:6-7)

in order to expose the serpent's lies? Did Jesus make up for sin, or did he expose the claims of sin?

3. Why is it fruitless for us to make up for our sins by way of created things? Are you comfortable with a concept of redemption whereby Christ made up for the sin of Adam?

4. What is the merit of the word "re-own" over the implications of the word "ransom"?

"To Be or Not to Be" (Holy, That Is)

WORD

"The LORD said to Moses, 'Speak to the whole Israelite community and tell them: Be holy, for I, the LORD, your God, am holy. Revere your mother and father, and keep my sabbaths. I, the LORD, am your God.

"Do not turn aside to idols, nor make molten gods for yourselves. I, the LORD, am your God'" (Lev 19:1-4).

REFLECTION

When we say, "God is holy," we are not predicating something about God as, for example, the man is tall, she is beautiful, the child is precocious, the community is alive. God's holiness is God's being. Should it be asked, "How does God be," the answer must be the one God ordered Moses to relate to the Israelite community: "I, the Lord your God, am holy." When God says, "I am holy," the reference is to divine existence, not to a divine possession.

God commanded the whole Israelite community to be holy because God is holy. Jesus issued this same invitation to his disciples. "In a word, you must be made perfect as your heavenly Father is perfect" (Matt 5:48). Holy hyperbole? Is it possible to become the essence of God? Are we offered the opportunity to say "I am holy" in the same way God says, "I, the Lord your God, am holy"? Is our being God's being?

77

By nature and by grace, we have been given the capacity to share in God's am-ness. We can be holy because our creaturehood has been given the capacity to be one with God and to share fully in God's life. What we call "spirituality" is not the process of becoming a divine being but of sharing in God's being, accessible to us through Jesus Christ and his redemptive mission.

We prepare for this mission of Christ by prayer, fasting, and almsgiving. These hallmarks of spirituality awaken our capacity to enflesh more fully God's being. It is by prayer, fasting, and almsgiving that the world's spirit not only loses its hold upon us but also loses its capacity to attract us. We are freed of the conviction that created goods possess a worth that transcends their creaturely purpose and value. When we experience this freedom, we are also ready to experience the being of the risen Christ and the being of God's am-ness, which transforms us.

Realizing that we share God's being generates within us an apostolic spirit. Holiness leads to mission. Through us, Christ carries on his mission of extending God's being to the poor. We will know that the being of God, holiness itself, is at work within our humanity when we begin to experience a hunger and thirst to work for justice. When a love for human dignity is at the center of our lives as it was at the center of Christ's, we will know that holiness is at the heart of our "I am," our authentic identity.

St. Leo writes: "No act of devotion on the part of the faithful gives God more pleasure than that which is lavished on the poor. Where he finds charity with its loving concern, there he recognizes the reflection of his own fatherly care."[18]

To be holy is to share with Christ his own concerns as he dwelt among us in the flesh. After his ascension into heaven, these concerns did not subside. The risen Christ, dwelling in the flesh and blood of the Church's members, is not less concerned for the plight of the poor. Holiness, God's being, becomes recognizable and felt as we hunger and thirst with a burning love for the poor.

In their pastoral "Economic Justice for All," the Catholic bishops of the United States write:

> Conversion is a lifelong process. And it is not undertaken alone. It occurs with the support of the whole believing community, through baptism, common prayer, and our daily efforts, large and small, on behalf of justice. As a Church we must be a people after God's own heart, bonded by the Spirit, sustaining one another in love, setting our hearts on God's kingdom, committing ourselves

to solidarity with those who suffer, working for peace and justice in the world. The Church cannot redeem the world from the deadening effects of sin and injustice in its own life and institutions. All of us must help the Church to practice in its own life what it preaches to others about economic justice and cooperation. . . .

Holiness is not limited to the sanctuary or to moments of private prayer; it is a call to direct our whole heart and life toward God and according to God's plan for the world.[19]

QUESTIONS FOR YOUR REFLECTION

1. If God invites us to be holy as God is holy, is this an invitation to be equal to God? Is our being holy the same as God's being is holy?

2. Holiness on our part is the fruit of a transformation, whereby we cooperate with the spirit of God to develop our graced capacity to share in the being of God. What is the role of prayer, fasting, and almsgiving in this transformation?

3. When we celebrate the Eucharist, we acknowledge that in, through, and with Christ we have already been made holy. Why, then, are we urged to pray, fast, and give alms as a spirituality that enables us to *become* holy? Is this a contradiction?

4. Why is an attraction to deeds of justice and compassion for the poor a sign of true holiness? What is the difference between do-goodism and the good works described by Jesus (see Matt 25:31-46) as criteria for final judgment?

Humanity: Worth Jesus?

WORD

> *"Moses said [to the Lord], 'The people around me include six hundred thousand soldiers; yet you say, "I will give them meat to eat for a whole month." Can enough sheep and cattle be slaughtered for them? If all the fish of the sea were caught for them, would they have enough?' The LORD answered Moses, 'Is this beyond the LORD's reach? You shall see now whether or not what I have promised you takes place'"* (Num 11:21-23).

REFLECTION

The Scriptures reveal a God who appears to be extravagant. God's generosity is such that one might be tempted at times to accuse God of boasting. What does one make of such statements as: "The LORD will give you meat, and you will eat it, not for one day, or two days, or five, or ten, or twenty days, but for a whole month—until it comes out of your very nostrils, and becomes loathsome to you." Or, "Is this beyond the LORD's reach?" (Num 11:18-20, 23)

The life of Jesus reveals even more the extravagance of God. St. Paul writes with astonishment as he exclaims, "He emptied himself and took the form of a slave" (Phil 2:7). Jesus told stories about extravagant love: the spendthrift son whose prodigal spending was matched only by his father's prodigal forgiveness (see Luke 15:11-32); the good Samaritan who not only attended to the immediate needs of a waylaid Jew but also provided funds for his future needs (see Luke 10:30-37); the master of the vineyard who paid the laborers hired at the end of the day the same wages as those hired at the beginning of the day (see Matt 20:1-16); the shepherd who left his flock of ninety-nine sheep in search of the one who was lost (see Luke 15:4-7).

Moreover, Jesus suggested forgiveness not seven times but seventy times seven times (see Matt 18:22); he suggested that the attentive Mary, not the Martha of many details, had chosen "the better portion" (Luke

10:41); he fed thousands with the rations of a small boy (see John 6:9); he suggested that his companions put out into the deep to reap a catch of fish that nearly swamped their boat (see Luke 5:4); he promised that those who followed him would "take [their] places on twelve thrones to judge the twelve tribes of Israel" (Matt 19:28); and he promised that "everyone who has given up home, brothers or sisters, father or mother, wife or children or property for my sake will receive many times as much and inherit everlasting life" (Matt 19:29).

What is to be said of this divine prodigality? Let's look at it this way: The extravagance of God is measured by the worth with which God appraises us, not by how *we* appraise value and worth. The price of God's appraisal is the Son of God sent to re-own us. That appraisal is of a worth indescribable, undefinable, and incomprehensible.

The reason God appears to be extravagant is that we simply do not have adequate tools to measure the love with which God appraises the priceless worth of human dignity. Nothing on this earth can be used to estimate and measure that worth except our humanity, with which the Son of God clothed himself. That is why the authors of Scripture had to struggle to express God's estimation of human worth. Every effort they made to show how much God loves our humanity turned out to be extravagant in terms of the tools we use to measure and evaluate.

We are left speechless, and that is as it should be. What word can we speak to express adequately our praise and thanksgiving? There is only one Word that can perfectly articulate God's love for human life. That Word is Jesus. Jesus is God's image, the image God created humanity to be like. Jesus is the worth of humanity, and his death on the cross is the evidence that no earthly word, no earthly reality, however noble, is sufficiently sovereign to be humanity's advocate before the throne of God. In him, through him, and with him, God was moved to raise up humanity and restore it to its original purpose.

Faith in the extravagance of God's love is a sign of our healthy faith in God. Can we really believe in God if we cannot bring ourselves to believe that our worth in his eyes has no limits? Do we not have here the remedy for the disease of poor self-esteem? Those who believe that they are worth the price of Christ's death and resurrection have a healthy faith in God. They also have a profound respect and reverence for their own self-worth. That's no exaggeration!

QUESTIONS FOR YOUR REFLECTION

1. In what way do humility and a healthy esteem of one's worth go hand in hand?

2. Why does poor self-esteem affect the quality of our faith in God?

3. Doing good works is one evidence of a healthy relationship with God. Is it possible, however, that a spirituality with heavy emphasis on good works and the merit that accrues from them might lead to egocentric self-esteem? Ultimately, what is it that justifies our favor with God and makes us right with God?

4. What does this mean: "Jesus is the worth of humanity and his death on the cross is the evidence that no earthly word, no earthly reality, however noble, is sufficiently sovereign to be humanity's advocate before the throne of God"?

No Cross, No Resurrection

WORD

"*The* LORD *said to Moses, 'Send men to reconnoiter the land of Canaan, which I am giving the Israelites.'*

"*After reconnoitering the land for forty days they . . . told Moses: 'We went into the land to which you sent us. It does indeed flow with milk and honey, and here is its fruit. However, the people who are living in the land are fierce, and the towns are fortified and very strong.'*

"*Caleb, however, to quiet the people toward Moses, said, 'We ought to go up and sieze the land, for we can certainly do so.' But the men who had gone up with him said, 'We cannot attack these people; they are too strong for us'*" (Num 13:1-2; 25-28; 30-31).

REFLECTION

The author of the Epistle to the Hebrews counsels, "Let us keep our eyes fixed on Jesus" (12:2).

We need to fix our eyes on Jesus crucified and on Jesus risen. To emphasize one over the other is to invite extremism. The dynamic of the Christian faith is the interaction of these two mysteries. This interaction is called the "paschal mystery," and it is central both to the redemptive mission of Jesus and to the meaning of human dignity and human identity.

The quality of faith with which we fix our eyes on Jesus is going to be determined by the attitudes we develop regarding human suffering and human purpose. Christians who, for one reason or another, do not understand the interaction of death and resurrection in terms of its necessity for human indentity will hardly be moved by the interaction of death and resurrection in the redemptive mission of Jesus. Their failure to accept suffering in their own humanity will scarcely motivate them to fix their eyes on a Messiah who accepted human suffering in order to redefine human purpose and re-own human identity. Christians who have defined their lives by a purpose other than the image and likeness they were created to become will have difficulty fixing their eyes on the Christ of the Gospels.

One of the reasons we fail to handle the ambiguity of dying and rising is the fallacy that every suffering and every loss must have at our disposal a clear explanation. In this regard, we are, ironically, victims of a marvelous technology that, in less than a hundred years, has grappled with and found solutions to problems formerly thought to be within the realm of God's miracles. Technology, of course, is filled with "miracles"—a tribute to the men and women whose dedication to the alleviation of human suffering is surely a source of hope for the future.

Unfortunately, the hopes of technology have tended to become a substitute for the gift of divine hope in terms of what people once expected of religion. When these hopes were encapsulated in the pills and caplets of technology, religion came to be regarded as a kind of spiritual paradise where suffering and failure are passé. We bring this attitude to Christ, and we fix our gaze only on the Christ of the resurrection. But what happens when neither technology nor religion provides answers? What happens when suffering and death stand before us in stony silence? What happens at the moment of death, when there are no answers except faith in a reality whose experience lies beyond our last breath?

Mysterious does not mean "unanswerable." It means "hidden." Mystery seeks to reveal its hiddenness, and in due time it will do so. The mysterious is unanswerable only to the extent that we refuse to pay the price of birth's pains—the pains that enable the unanswerable to be delivered from its hiddenness.

Pilgrims must live with ambiguity. The Israelites who hungered and thirsted for the fruits of the Promised Land shrank back, however, when the conquest of those fruits posed what seemed to them an insurmountable barrier. The Israelites had gladly fled into the desert to escape their Egyptian slavery. But when they experienced the desert, they seemed eager to flee both the desert and their freedom for the fleshpots of Egypt. They deemed the desert experience too great a price to pay for God's gift of hope.

To fix our eyes on Jesus is to fix our gaze on the death-resurrection ambiguity of our humanity. The uniqueness of Christ's life was that he revealed the redemptive nature of suffering. What does this mean? It means that in the mystery of death-resurrection, Christ revealed his solidarity with our suffering as the ultimate judgment against the lie that humanity can compete with the lordship of God.

Similarly, we do not know precisely how the resurrection will take place in us. That's not important. What is important is to recognize that ambiguity and failure are not synonomous. Faith can flourish in an environment of unanswerables. In that environment, Christ's risen humanity offers hope for those whose hearts have the capacity to transcend the horizons of what they can't humanly answer.

Christ is the Messiah. We can never become a messianic people until we are ready to place our hope in a newness of humanity that lies infinitely beyond and above technology's answers to humanity's earth-bound questions. We become messianic when we are ready to suffer for a hope that has already charged the world "with the grandeur of God" but has not yet flamed out "like shining from shook foil" (Hopkins).[20] We may not yet be able to fix our eyes on the "shining," but we can fix our eyes on the hope of a grandeur hidden within a creation groaning for our gaze.

QUESTIONS FOR YOUR REFLECTION

1. What are the unanswerables in your life? Have they diminished your faith? Have they helped your faith grow?

2. In terms of your own human identity, why is suffering necessary? Can you cite a discovery about your identity that came about as a result of an unanswerable with which you were (or are) forced to grapple?

3. In what respect has technology crippled our patience and our ability to let the hiddenness of truth reveal itself at its own pace?

4. Why is learning to live with unanswerables a good way to prepare for death?

Fidelity to Covenant: Prayer's Power

WORD

> " 'Now then, let the power of my Lord be displayed in
> its greatness, even as you have said, "The LORD is slow to
> anger and rich in kindness, forgiving wickedness and crime." '
>
> "The LORD answered: 'I pardon them as you have
> asked' " (Num 14:17-18, 20).

REFLECTION

The power of intercessory prayer is not derived from human gifts of persuasiveness, moral rectitude, or ascetical practices. One stands in God's presence righteous before ethical, doctrinal, and ritual credentials are required. We are reminded that it was the sinful publican who returned to his home righteous rather than the fully credentialed Pharisee (see Luke 18:9-14). One stands before God righteous by way of a covenanted promise from which God will never back away.

The power of Moses' prayer of intercession in behalf of a stubborn people sprang from his fidelity to God's word. Moses defended his people in terms of the power of God's word, by which he had been formed. God heard not the words spoken by Moses but the witness of Moses' transformation. The covenant written on tablets of stone was not a contract with God. It had been written on the heart of Moses. God pardoned the stubbornness of the people on the strength of that irrevocable Word carved in Moses' being.

The Word of God became flesh and, in the blessed incarnation of Jesus Christ, became available to all of us. God's Word in Christ is God's Word made flesh, dwelling among us forever. Raised up by God once and for all on Easter Sunday and dwelling among us who are his flesh and blood, the Word of God forms us and empowers our prayers of intercession before God. Our prayers move God not on the strengths of our moral accomplishments, our doctrinal orthodoxy, or our ritual preciseness, praiseworthy though these credentials be. Our prayers move God because they are prayed in Christ, through Christ, and with Christ. Christ is irrevocably written in our hearts.

Jesus is the final and the ultimate covenant of God and people. God is faithful to us, and Jesus is God's testimony of divine faithfulness. Jesus became a human being because God created humanity worthy of that incarnation. Intercessory prayer becomes powerful when it is offered not from reasons we consider justifiable but from a capacity for a justice already promised us by God. If, then, God's Word has been welcomed into the depths of our own personhood and allowed to form, shape, and seal our identity with the indelible character and identity of Christ's own wordness, our intercessory prayer takes on the character of Christ's prayer.

Some of the conditions for discipleship are that we pray for our enemies, that we beg forgiveness for those who have injured us, and that we forgive "seventy times seven times" (Matt 18:22). We are to offer intercessory prayer because the indwelling presence of Christ, God's Word and covenant, empowers prayer to bring about reconciliation and peace between ourselves and our enemies. This doesn't make praying for our enemies easier, but it is a challenge to our faith and the covenanted faithfulness we are called to make in response to God's covenanted fidelity.

When the Word of God informs, forms, and *trans*forms our identity, prayer has been effective. We are to believe not so much in the weight of our prayers but in the weight of God's glory, which justifies our prayers. The weight of that glory enables us to see as God sees. This is faith, and it is this faith that justifies God's response to our intercessions. For if we pray in Christ, we pray for what Christ prays in us. To be in communion with this prayer is the power of intercessory prayer.

QUESTIONS FOR YOUR REFLECTION

1. Before anything else, prayer is the openness of our hearts to God. When prayer really opens our hearts, what is the risk we run? (I use the word "risk" with tongue in cheek.)

2. The more intimate we become with God's Word, the more certain we can be that what we pray for will be according to God's will. Can you give a reason for this line of thought?

3. In the parable of the Pharisee and the publican, each offered God a credential. For the Pharisee, it was the contract of deeds done. For the publican, it was trust in God's covenant. Do you find this contract-versus-covenant tension at work in you as you endeavor

to define your stance before God? Are you, from time to time, in one corner or the other?

4. How is prayer for people who ordinarily "drive me up a wall" a sign that discipleship is taking shape in your life?

Freedom and Human Development

WORD

"Constituted as the Lord by his resurrection, Christ, to whom all power in heaven and on earth has been given, is still at work in the hearts of men through the power of his Spirit. Not only does he awaken in them a longing for the world to come, but by that very fact he also inspires and strengthens those generous desires by which the human family seeks to make its own life more human and to achieve the same goal for the whole world.

"The gifts of the Spirit are manifold. He calls some to bear open witness to the longing for a dwelling place in heaven, and to keep this fresh in the minds of all mankind; he calls others to dedicate themselves to the service of men here upon earth, preparing by this ministry the material for the kingdom of heaven.

"Yet he makes all free, so that, by denying their love of self and taking up all earth's resources into the life of man, all may reach out to the future, when humanity itself will become an offering acceptable to God" (The Church in the Modern World).[21]

REFLECTION

We are free when we become conscious of the fuller identity hidden in the inexhaustible mystery of our undisclosed selves. The restlessness and the longing we experience can never be silenced simply by the pursuit of having. This is not to say that having this world's goods makes them less good, nor are we less free by possessing them. But it is to say that having, possessing, and owning are not the determinants of freedom, nor are they the determinants of human meaning and identity.

We are free and we are human when we are liberated from the illusion that identity is determined by what we have. We are loveable not because we have possessions but because we have been liberated from the narrow identity by which our preoccupation with possessions defines us. We are loved when a loved one motivates us to pursue the moreness of personhood hidden within the depths of our inner selves. That moreness lies in the infinite creator, whose image and likeness was the reason for humanity's existence.

Sinfulness springs from the brokenness that isolates egos from selves. The unhappy person is the one who is trapped within the narrow boundaries of ego esteem. This entrapment generates never-ending longings that demand satisfaction. The result? Identity crises. If one's choice of this world's goods is the reason for ultimate existence, the chooser can expect an inflated ego. But if one opts for human development, that is, the pursuit of one's heretofore undisclosed self, one can expect the joy of what it means to become human: the assuagement of never-ending thirsts for ego esteem and the freedom to be the sharer of God's identity.

Human development is our first vocation. When we are loved to the point of thirsting for a fuller disclosure of who we are, we can be confident that we have begun the journey toward our priceless destiny. The one who truly loves us sends us on a journey of self-discovery to find the moreness of self and, ultimately, God.

Ego knowledge is necessary. Who I know myself to be is good. Who I know myself to be, however, is not all I am. If ego is all I am, then the longings to become fully human will be silenced by the longings for the self-indulgence of a never-satisfied egocentricity. These cravings will seek their satisfaction in the pursuit of things whose identity can never measure up to the image and likeness divinely envisioned for a developing humanity. When having, possessing, and owning are synonymous with human identity, we pursue dehumanization. We miss the mark of creation's purpose.

We cannot be free or human simply because we have everything we want. We are free when we are enabled to begin the journey into our hidden selves, and we love others when we challenge them to a similar pursuit. Such a labor of love does not still the longings for happiness, but it does channel them toward the direction of integrity. To seek out the self-identity hidden in the mystery of our humanness silences those ego cravings that do nothing for us except generate more cravings. Surely we are not free if we cannot be liberated from this vicious circle. The goods of this world will always be good because they are gifts of God. But they cannot possibly still the cries of restless hearts craving to become the image and likeness of God.

QUESTIONS FOR YOUR REFLECTION

1. Can you recall any person who motivated you to explore an aspect of your identity you were formerly unaware of? What part of the reflection rings true in terms of your relationship with that person?

2. When do you feel truly free? When do you feel unfree? As you answer each question, do you observe any connection between your answer and the issue of human development?

3. Do you see any connection between becoming human and becoming one with God? Is there a connection between "holy" and "wholly"?

4. What was the biggest surprise you ever received about yourself? Did the discovery free you? Did it lead to a change in the way you live?

5. Why does becoming human awaken "a longing for the world to come" (see "Word" above)? What is the connection?

More than Script or Sound

WORD

"In times past, God spoke in fragmentary and varied ways to our fathers through the prophets; in this, the final age, he has spoken to us through his Son, whom he has made heir of all things and through whom he first created the universe. This Son is the reflection of the Father's glory, the exact representation of the Father's being" (Heb 1:1-3).

REFLECTION

The Word of God is more than script or sound. The Word is God's power and God's presence made flesh in the person of Jesus Christ. The Son of God was not sent to speak to us *about* the Father. Jesus *is* the power and the presence of the Father, "the exact representation of the Father's being" (see "Word" above), dwelling among us not in some fragmentary and varied way but as the fullness of who God is.

Word made flesh, Jesus embodied the creative power of God. Jesus graced our humanity with that same creative power and presence. Our participation in the wordness of the Son of God graces us to share the prophetic power and presence of Christ. Just as Christ came as the exact representation of the Father's being, so we who make up his body here on earth are endowed with both the privilege and the responsibility of representing the Father's being.

With the coming of Christ, the prophetic role became more than "speaking words" for God. The incarnate life of Jesus literally *spoke* God. Jesus did not come among us to give lectures about the Father. As Jesus was sent to be the exact representation of the Father, so Jesus sent the Holy Spirit into the world at Pentecost to grace the disciples with the capacity to be that graced representation. As the Father's advocate, the Holy Spirit empowered the Church to become the graced advocate of the Father in the world—the prophetic voice of the Father's Word. Gifted by the Holy Spirit to be the wordness of Jesus, the Church speaks God with the power and the presence of the Word of God in the world.

91

What the Church speaks will differ radically from the message of the world. The Church, as the prophetic voice of Jesus, will always take "the road less traveled." There's the difference. The Church speaks of justice and human dignity and calls out to all the beggars entombed in the sepulchers of injustice and indignity: "Lazarus, come out!" (John 11:43) How different this call from the world's babbling calls for self-glorification! Even though the Church must be ready to be persecuted and denounced, may she be consoled to know that her difference was noticed. Eventually, her difference comes to be accepted as her identity and, ultimately, the guarantee of followship.

To be endowed with the wordness of Christ is to be sealed with the responsibility of making the world better. As bearers of the Word, we are a "sent" people, gifted to share with Christ and his Father the ongoing creation of a better world. We have been given the gift of life in Christ not to be excused from responsibilities to the world but to grace it with the presence and the power of the Word made flesh. Jesus was emphatic when he said that he was sent into the world not to condemn it but to save it (see John 3:17). To share in the wordness of Jesus is to respond to one's fundamental vocation of discipleship. As the embodiment of God's Word here on earth, we have the responsibility of speaking God, of being the prophetic voice of God's Word. The fact that this voice will not often be received favorably does not excuse us from the responsibility of speaking.

Jesus did not use the excuse of Lazarus' entombment to escape the responsibility of calling him forth from the power of death. Jesus accepted the mission to be the exact representation of the Father's power and presence. As God's Word, the power and the presence of God called Lazarus forth from the tomb. We are disciples of Jesus when we, too, stand before the tombs of this world's "dead" speaking the wordness of Jesus, which we have been baptized, sealed, and sent to speak. We are not called to put our faith in the success of what we endeavor to call forth. We are called to be *faithful* to the mission of our baptism—to re-present again and again God's power and presence.

QUESTIONS FOR YOUR REFLECTION

1. What is the difference between knowing about God and experiencing the power and the presence of God? Which of the two casts the members of the Church in a prophetic role? What do you mean by "prophetic role"?

2. Pope Paul VI writes: "Modern man listens more willingly to witnesses than to teachers, and if he listens to teachers it is because they are witnesses."[22] What is the difference between a witness and a teacher?

3. Why must the Church's authenticity rest, among other things, upon her prophetic stance? Give examples of ways that the Church evidences positions radically different from those of other institutions and corporate bodies.

4. One might think that the Church's differences would turn more people away. History shows that the Church's prophetic stance eventually attracts people. Why is this?

5. How can an ordinary person exercise the responsibility of speaking God in today's world? Give an example of one who literally spoke God to you with his or her life. How do you think you speak God? Do you think that, because you are a Catholic, your life is radically different from others'? How?

MONDAY OF THE FIFTH WEEK

Too Good to Be True?

WORD

"Now, since the children are men [and women] of blood and flesh, Jesus likewise had a full share in ours, that by his death he might rob the devil, the prince of death, of his power, and free those who through fear of death had been slaves their whole life long. [Jesus] had to become like his brothers [and sisters] in every way, that he might be a merciful and faithful high priest before God on their behalf, to expiate the sins of the people" (Heb 2:14-17).

REFLECTION

The terror of death can be greatly minimized if we really believe that Jesus' death put to death Satan's power to make us slaves of death.

This liberating truth of our faith can erase death's terror and inspire us with the longing for eternal life.

To understand more fully the effect of Christ's redemptive activity with its devastating blow to death, we need to catch the implications of what is meant by "Christ's full share in our blood and flesh." Christ's redemption was a catastrophic blow to Satan because Jesus became what the prince of darkness can never become. He became a human being.

To become human means to embrace human purpose. That purpose is to be like God. Think of it! He who was by nature God surrendered himself so completely to human nature that he entered the human process of becoming like God. "He had become like his brothers [and sisters] in every way" (see "Word" above).

The incarnation was a devastating blow to Satan because Christ restored to humanity the way to its purpose. Jesus came into the world as the way God created *us* to be human. By emptying himself of equality with the Father, he showed humanity its glory—creaturehood. Embracing our creaturehood as fully as possible was the way Jesus put death to death. Not to know this way had been the real terror of death.

Jesus unmasked the serpent's lie, "You certainly will not die [for] God knows well that the moment you eat of [the tree of the knowledge of good and bad] your eyes will be opened" (Gen 3:4-5). To Adam and Eve, the serpent claimed for humanity an equality from sources other than God. The lie? God's sovereign creatorship was not the way to human destiny and purpose. Humanity was created to receive God's love and, through that love, to become the image and likeness of the creator. Was God's claim too good to be true for Adam and Eve? Well, they fell for the lie.

Christ, the second Adam, came into the world to restate a truth that is *not* too good to be true. It was precisely in humanity's created aptitude for God-likeness that Jesus found kinship with us. He destroyed forever the lie that God-likeness is achieved through the possession of this world's fruits. He left Satan demolished for the simple reason that Satan could in no way relate to humanity's God-given purpose of existence. Jesus became human in every way except sin, while Satan could become human in no way except the possibility of sin.

Death still terrifies because we cannot bring ourselves to believe the good news that Satan is powerless. We sin not because sin is still alive before God but because we feel more comfortable being alive before lesser gods. Conversion is the gift to embrace the truth that Jesus still lives sovereignly within our graced capacity to become like God. We sin because we really aren't persuaded of the presence of God's power within us. We are already graced to be saved, but our courage is not such as to embrace fully that astonishing truth.

Satan no longer has the capacity to destroy us. Yet we fear death—not because we don't believe God raised Jesus from death but because we can't seem to bring ourselves to believe that God has raised us too. What is really terrifying is our reluctance to believe that death's power is dead because the sin of creaturehood's sovereignty is dead. What's still alive is Satan's pitch that our resurrection is too good to be true.

QUESTIONS FOR YOUR REFLECTION

1. What, for you, is the most terrifying aspect of death?

2. St. Paul tells us that "Christ emptied himself, not deeming equality with God something to be grasped at" (see Phil 2:6-7). At the moment of death, of what are we emptied that brings us terror? Is faith in that which we cannot imagine also part of the terror?

3. Grace builds on nature, it is said. In what way does sin endanger that truth? What, precisely, was the lie of Satan's promises (see Gen 3:1-7; Matt 4:1-11; Luke 4:1-13)?

4. The agony of death is but the birth pangs of eternal life. Isn't it true that the seeming finality of death's agony deprives us of the expectancy of death's birth pangs? Have you ever reflected on death as the pains of our birth into eternal life?

Be Careful of the Gods on Whom You Fix Your Gaze

WORD

> *"Fix your eyes on Jesus, the apostle and high priest whom we acknowledge in faith, who was faithful to him who appointed him.*
>
> *"Take care, . . . lest any of you have an evil and unfaithful spirit and fall away from the living God. Encourage one another daily while it is still 'today,' so that no one grows hardened by the deceit of sin. We have become partners of Christ only if we maintain to the end that confidence with which we began"* (Heb 3:1-2, 12-14).

REFLECTION

"Sacrifice" means "to make holy." Unfortunately, this is not the meaning we give it. What probably leaps to our minds when we hear the word is an image of something slain, abandoned, or given up for a greater good.

There is no doubt that these images accompany sacrificial acts. If holiness of life is to be realized, something of our lives that has kept us from holiness needs to be slain, abandoned, and given up. What is unfortunate is that these negative marks of sacrifice are often perceived as the only meaning of sacrifice. This prevents us from understanding why Jesus regarded the cross as his glory.

To fix our eyes on Jesus is to fix them on his cross as the indispensable means of experiencing the full glory of the resurrection. "How great beyond all telling the glory of the passion," writes St. Leo the Great in one of his homilies.[23] The cross of Christ put to death the power of the serpent's lie to rob humanity of its wholeness and its holiness. The sacrifice of Jesus left naked the serpent's blatant boast, "You will be like gods" (Gen 3:5), leaving God free to raise up humanity to the righteousness and justice that human nature claims by its right to be like God.

The passion of Christ is the "judgment seat" of the Lord not in the sense of condemnation but as a measure of God's esteem, that through Christ's passion, human understanding might begin to esteem the value of human worth. In the desert, Christ had already repudiated values unworthy of the purpose of human creation. With eyes fixed on his Father, he had been able to see God's glory as relatable to humanity's graced capacity to reclaim that glory. The cross of Jesus was humanity's glory because Jesus' death exposed the lie that the things of this world are the ultimate glory of being human. No earthly savior was around to raise up Jesus after he died. The immeasurable love of the Father raised up Jesus and the humanity his presence dignified. Jesus' sacrificial death on the cross brought forth the power of God's will to make holy and re-own the humanity God judged to be holy from the first moment of creation.

The Lord's passion and death condemned the world not as a place but as a spirit contrary to God's plan of creation. The plan of God did not include sovereignty of the world as the pinnacle of human existence. The Father raised up Jesus to proclaim again that human fulfillment arises out of a purpose transcending the goodness and beauty of the world. Christ's death on the cross was not a condemnation of the world's goodness and beauty. Christ died on the cross to condemn the serpent's lie that the world's beauty and goodness contain the ultimate purpose for human existence.

Jesus' death proclaimed the utter futility of the world's spirit as the supreme goal of human existence. As Jesus hung on the cross, humankind could, at last, begin to see the meaning of Adam and Eve's discovery of their nakedness (see Gen 3:7). What they had been induced to possess as the supreme goal of life stripped them of the dignity of who they were created to become. No earthly possession, however good and beautiful it was created to be, was around to save Jesus from death when he hung on the tree. Why? Because the spirit of this world's claim of sovereignty is without substance. It can't deliver what it boasts. Trees, the serpent boasted, had the power to make Adam and Eve like gods. That boast vanished when Christ hung from one.

The cross became the formless wasteland awaiting a new creation at the hands of God's sovereignty (see Gen 1:2). In the wilderness experience of Christ's death the Father raised up a new humanity, sealed with Christ's sacrificial guarantee that the way of Satan had been sealed off and the way to holiness reopened. The death and resurrection of Jesus re-owned humanity for God because Christ exposed the futility of Satan's way. Christ's way opened for sinners the escape route so that they might flee the bonds of death and become relinked with the source of all life.

QUESTIONS FOR YOUR REFLECTION

1. Holiness is not a thing with which God rewards us for deeds well done. Rather, it is the transformation of one's personhood. How does sacrifice relate to that transformation?

2. Why does authentic holiness demand that we fix our eyes on Jesus? How does that translate in your life?

3. The glory of God is the mystery of God's resurrection in the depths of each person's mystery. Why is the passion and death of Christ an integral part of God's glory? What is meant by "paschal mystery"?

4. A TV beer commercial proclaims, "It doesn't get any better than this!" How does this commercial and its gospel reflect the spirit of the world? In what way is this spirit contrary to the spirit of Christ? What are the parameters of each?

In Heaven as It Is on Earth

WORD

"God could give no greater gift to men than to make his Word, through whom he created all things, their head and to join them to him as his members, so that the Word might be both Son of God and son of man, one God with the Father, and one man with all men.

"He prays for us as our priest, he prays in us as our head, he is the object of our prayers as our God. Let us then recognize both our voice in his, and his voice in ours. Our thoughts must then be awakened to keep their vigil of faith. We must realize that the one whom we were contemplating . . . in his nature as God took to himself the nature of a servant; he was made in the likeness of men and found to be a man like others; he humbled himself by being obedient even to accepting death; as he hung on the cross he made the psalmist's words his own: 'My God, my God, why have you forsaken me?' [Matt 27:46]" (St. Augustine, bishop)[24]

REFLECTION

St. John writes in his Gospel prologue: "In the beginning was the Word; and the Word was in God's presence, and the Word was God. He was present to God in the beginning. Through him all things came into being, and apart from him nothing came to be" (1:1-3). Here, St. John makes known a relationship between God and the Word revealing the closest possible communion.

He reveals this communion between the Father and the Son not because he must defend the authenticity of the Word's sonship but because he wants us to consider the graced communion that exists between God's Word and our humanity. The evangelist's prologue is not a history lesson about the beginnings of Jesus. Rather, it is the setting for the amazing truth that divinity and humanity belong together in a communion like the communion of Father and Son.

How beautifully John draws the parallel of Christ's oneness with the Father and his oneness with humanity. On the one hand, "The Word was in God's presence and the Word was God" (John 1:1). On the other hand, "The Word became flesh and made his dwelling among us" (John 1:14). Just as the Word's eternal presence with the Father inspired John to write, "and the Word was God," so the Word's coming among us inspired him to write, "The Word became flesh and made his dwelling among us."

Consider the implications! Jesus the Christ who is by nature the Word of God stands before the Father bearing the stamp of our human nature. How authentically he is able to articulate the deepest groans of all people!

And so, communion with the Word of God carries with it the guarantee that our groans and griefs bear the seal of Christ's own character. Our cries of anguish are not aimless pleadings uttered as if, perchance, a far-away God out there in the darkness may be listening. Our communion with the Word of God is such that as we speak Christ speaks and as Christ speaks we speak. "He prays for us as our priest, he prays in us as our head, he is the object of our prayers as our God. Let us then recognize both our voice in his, and his voice in ours" (see "Word" above). Jesus is God's Word to us from the Father, and he is the Word from us to the Father.

But there is yet another implication. The author of the Epistle to the Hebrews writes: "God is not unjust; he will not forget your work and the love you have shown him by your service, past and present, to his holy people" (6:10). Our union with the Word empowers us to be a priestly people and to mediate Christ as we witness communion with Christ before God's people. When our work and love are done in Christ or when we pray in Christ, we enable the Holy Spirit to render the power and the presence of God's Word truly effective. In Christ, God has kept his Word. Jesus is the oath by which God swears fidelity to his promises. God does not forget even one act of love done in the name of Christ, because the character of Christ is forever sealed on our humanity.

Christ is the guarantee that God does not lie. God gave us the Word and that Word was faithful unto death itself. The Word was sent to reveal the lie of Satan's word. He who was sovereign emptied himself of that sovereignty so that he who lied about human sovereignty might be forever exposed by the Word of truth. God kept the divine oath when Jesus was raised up, enabling all of humanity to keep forever the sovereignty of God's communion with us.

QUESTIONS FOR YOUR REFLECTION

1. Why do divinity and humanity belong together? In what way is the sacrament of Holy Communion a proclamation of this belonging?

2. Each human being is unique. Why is it imperative that Christ share in each person's sufferings? In the Epistle to the Colossians, St. Paul writes that our sufferings "fill up what is lacking in the sufferings of Christ" (1:24). In terms of Christ's relationship to humankind, what was "lacking" in his sufferings?

3. When a person says, "I kept my word," what is meant? How is Jesus the kept Word of the Father? Explain how Jesus is the eternal faithfulness of the Father's covenant. By the same token, how can we become the eternal faithfulness of humanity?

4. We turn to Mary the Mother of God as an example of humanity's vertical communion with God as well as its horizontal communion with one another. Can you identify this twofold communion in the stories of the annunciation (see Luke 1:26-38) and the visitation (see Luke 1:39-45)?

Melchizedek Who?

WORD

"See the greatness of [Melchizedek] to whom Abraham the patriarch gave one tenth of his booty! The law provides that the priests of the tribe of Levi should receive tithes from the people, their brother Israelites, even though all of them are descendants of Abraham; but Melchizedek, who was not of their ancestry, received tithes of Abraham and blessed him who had received God's promises" (Heb 7:4-6).

REFLECTION

As Jesus was the Messiah sent by God, so the Church is a messianic people sent by Jesus. "As the Father has sent me, so I send you" (John 20:21). To be messianic is yet another implication of the incarnation, which empowers us to experience the communion of divinity and humanity.

What is meant by "messianic people"? In *The Emergent Church*, Johann Metz writes:

> When the Church . . . repeats the messianic sayings regarding the reign of God and the future disclosed therein, it is speaking primarily in this case to people who already possess a future. They bring their own future, as it were, into the Church with them—the powerful and unshakably optimistic to have it religiously endorsed and uplifted, the fearful to have it protected and confirmed by religion. In this way, the messianic future frequently becomes a ceremonial elevation and transfiguration of a bourgeois future already worked out elsewhere. . . . In the Christianity of our time, the messianic religion of the Bible has largely been changed into bourgeois religion.[25]

Metz is not denouncing the middle class as such, nor does he denounce the possession of this world's goods. What concerns him is the tendency to regard economic and social success as credentials for God's endorsement of a future that middle-class attitudes have already formed and shaped. The middle class take their success to sanctuaries of religion in order to receive religion's seal of approval for a messianic identity defined by the middle class. "The real danger [of this 'bourgeois religion'] is [that it endorses and reinforces] those who already have . . . abundant prospects and a rich future."[26]

What qualifies us to be a messianic people is not the evidence of our success as the standard for a spiritually secure future but the evidence of a human-divine relationship *God* has designed for the future. Those who point to their possessions as the irrefutable sign of God's approval are walking into the future not as a messianic people but as a people whose success has them believing that God really does turn stones into bread.

The spirit of poverty is endorsed and blessed by Christ because the poor in spirit are qualified to enter a future not defined by this world's possessions. Nothing of this world determines messianic status. It is the sovereignty of God that disrupts all pretense of earthly sovereignty to proclaim the lordship of God's kingdom on earth.

Coming, so to speak, out of nowhere, Melchizedek is the symbol of the utter newness and transcendence of God's messiahship. Abraham's blessing by Melchizedek was outside the framework of Levitical propriety, custom, and protocol. This blessing revealed the depths of Abraham's hope. The king of Salem, like the Christ he prefigured, symbolized a priesthood that invited Abraham and his people to a future not defined by any earthly credential. Abraham received Melchizedek's blessing as if to acknowledge that its hope carried him beyond the sanctions of prescribed rituals.

We are a priestly, messianic people when, poor in spirit, we choose to pin our hope on the Messiah, who leads us into a future he will define. Christ called for the formation of a new people whose messianic identity would flow from a wisdom "eye has not seen, ear has not heard" (1 Cor 2:9).

The Fathers of the Second Vatican Council call us to venerate Christ as the lasting and sure seed of unity:

> This messianic people, although it does not actually include all . . . , and may more than once look like a small flock, is nonetheless a lasting and sure seed of unity, hope, and salvation for the whole human race. Established by Christ as a fellowship of life, charity, and truth, it is also used by him as an instrument for the redemption of all, and is sent forth into the whole world as the light of the world and the salt of the earth [see Matt 5:13-16].[27]

QUESTIONS FOR YOUR REFLECTION

1. When the followers of Jesus referred to him as "Messiah," what messianic image did they have in mind (see Matt 16:13-20)? After Peter declared that Jesus was the Messiah, why did Jesus come down hard on Peter (see Matt 16:22-24)? Why did the death of Jesus on the cross reflect God's standards about messiahship rather than human standards?

2. What do you think is the prevailing attitude about failure among people with whom you associate? Reflecting on your past life, what has been your attitude toward failure?

3. Listing some of the problems the Church faces today, could you make the case that God is calling the Church to experience the spirit of poverty so that she might more clearly reveal her messianic nature? Do these problems diminish Christian hope? Don't they enable hope to be more clearly discernible?

4. Very often we use the word "hope" when we mean "wish." For example, "I hope I get a promotion" is really a wish. What is hope? In what way is hope a certainty? Why is the spirit of poverty a necessity for a clearer understanding of Christian hope?

The Wider Vistas of Priesthood

WORD

"If perfection had been achieved through the levitical priesthood (on the basis of which the people received the law), what need would there have been to appoint a priest according to the order of Melchizedek, instead of choosing a priest according to the order of Aaron? When there is a change of priesthood, there is necessarily a change of law. Now he of whom these things are said was of a different tribe, none of whose members ever officiated at the altar. It is clear that our Lord rose from the tribe of Judah, regarding which Moses said nothing about priests" (Heb 7:11-14).

REFLECTION

Among Catholics, priesthood has been frequently understood solely within the context of holy orders, just as among Jews, it was understood solely within the context of its Levitical origins. This is not to say that priesthood is without special and distinct meaning within this context. When, however, priesthood is perceived solely within the context of holy orders, it comes to have meaning only in terms of priestly roles and functions. Hence, large numbers of people tend to perceive themselves outside the parameters of a much larger perception of priesthood whose origin is the sacrament of baptism.

Although all are not called to be ordained, all are called to participate in the transformation of humanity, which the sacrament of baptism signifies and the sacrament of holy orders celebrates and enables. Would not priesthood be more clearly understood if it were discussed in terms of its capacity to mediate and reveal God, which is the mission of the Church? Both ordained priests and laity are mandated to engage in this work because both share the human frame of reference that gives priestliness an important credential.

Priesthood as mediation has, in Christ, prior existence to the sacrament of holy orders because Jesus Christ the high priest identified himself with our humanity. This identity laid the groundwork for the

105

institution of the sacrament of holy orders. Baptism calls humanity to its mediating role. Holy orders celebrates the good news that mediation is a possibility for humanity. Baptism exalts the dignity of holy orders and the dignity of those who respond to its calling.

When the sacraments of baptism and holy orders are linked, the purpose is not to water down or make vague the meaning of ministerial priesthood. The clarity of ministerial priesthood has been diminished precisely because the two sacraments have not been linked. Because of their separation, the ministry of God's transforming works, to which baptism invites *all* men and women, has become the sole prerogative of a select few ordained priests and deacons.

When we ask, "What are the transforming, priestly works of Jesus," the author of the Epistle to the Hebrews suggests that we "keep our eyes fixed on Jesus" (12:2). Those who have their eyes fixed on Jesus learn that, above all, Jesus is the model of reconciliation. On the other hand, those of God's chosen people who did not follow Jesus considered the works of the Law to be a source of alienation between themselves and Jesus. In their eyes, religion excluded those whose lives were marked with sickness and suffering. For Jesus, discipleship did not call for adherence to code, creed, and cult as the *only* means of salvation.

Jesus willingly and generously shared his priesthood with all whose companionship took him into ghettos of brokenness created by an adherence to code, creed, and cult "salvation." Jesus came into the world to proclaim the good news that solidarity with God springs not from humanly designed guarantees of salvation but from a human dignity conferred upon all men and women created to be in the image and likeness of God.

Jesus did not condemn the priestly tribe of Levites who carried out priestly functions related to code, creed, and cult. However, his vision of priesthood included what he deemed to be the basic requirements of discipleship. When, for example, Jesus commanded Peter to forgive seventy times seven times, he spoke to Peter neither as a Levite nor as an ordained priest from Galilee but as a disciple whose humanity had been graced to share in Jesus' own transforming work of reconciliation of all who accepted the responsibility of discipleship.

The never-ending task of forgiveness and reconciliation is a role not confined to a tiny portion of ordained priests. It is the realm of all who have been baptized to lead a life of discipleship. Baptism calls us to a discipleship that enables us to live according to the image and likeness of God, an image and likeness that had been mediated for us through God's Son, and in whom God's divinity and our humanity have been reconciled. The good news? All who have been baptized share in this mission of reconciliation.

Who, then, are those ordained to the ministry of priesthood? Ordained priests are called to be sacraments of Christ's way of living, into which baptism initiates us. They are also called by the Church's sacrament of holy orders to minister the sacraments, which make efficacious those powers all disciples are expected to witness. The ordained priest assembles people, challenges them, and celebrates with them the transformation God longs to carry out in, with, and through them. He calls, challenges, and celebrates not because God's transforming works are the priest's alone to do here upon earth but because he is a living sacrament of what the "royal priesthood" (see 1 Pet 2:9) means, the priesthood that includes all of the faithful. Ordained priests call all men and women to remember that they, too, share in God's transforming works of reconciliation.

The shrinkage of priests' numbers and of the numbers of students studying for the ministerial priesthood today is not evidence that ordained priests are no longer needed or that the priesthood of the baptized laity has reached a point of maturity making ordained priesthood obsolete. It may well be that fewer priests are evidence that priesthood understood only in terms of the sacrament of holy orders has made ordained priesthood seem less imperative and, therefore, in danger of becoming less attractive.

A child who has been influenced by a priestly, eucharistic way of living among those with whom he has shared his life is more likely to be attracted to a way of living that involves an ordained ministry. Should he be attracted to the sacrament of holy orders and be ordained, he brings to that ordination a priestly way of life already experienced in a faith community. He has become an ordained priest because he has felt chosen to choose this way of life. This could not have been, however, unless he first experienced being an integral part of "a chosen race, a royal priesthood, a holy nation, a people he claims for his own" (1 Pet 2:9).

QUESTIONS FOR YOUR REFLECTION

1. When ordained priests forgive penitents sacramentally, how do penitents give witness to the sacramentality of that priestly ministry? How do penitents "enflesh" the ministry of ordained priests?

2. Ordained priests are absolutely necessary for the valid and efficacious celebrations of the sacraments of Eucharist and reconciliation.
At what point, however, can sacramental ministry have the appearances of superstition, magic, and theatrical performance? What of
priesthood's wider scope needs to be included to enrich ministerial
priesthood's substance and meaning?

3. What needs to be seriously considered by those who constitute "a
chosen race, a royal priesthood, a holy nation, a people he claims
for his own" (1 Pet 2:9), when it is obvious that the sacraments in
which they participate leave much to be desired in terms of their
effects? Isn't there much to be desired in situations where parents
want their children to be baptized but want parish catechists to be
entirely responsible for their children's faith and religious education?

4. How would you explain this: "God calls all the baptized to be sacraments of the sacraments"?

SATURDAY OF THE FIFTH WEEK

Ah! Sweet Mystery of Life

WORD

> "So let us take our part in the Passover. . . . We must
> sacrifice ourselves to God, each day and in everything we
> do, accepting all that happens to us for the sake of the Word,
> imitating his passion by our sufferings, and honoring his
> blood by shedding our own. We must be ready to be cruci-
> fied" (St. Gregory Nazianzen, bishop).[28]

REFLECTION

The Church frequently refers to mysteries of faith not only as doctrines of faith inviting our assent but also as the relivable events of
Christ's life inviting our consent. These mysteries of faith are not mere
historical conversation pieces to be discussed throughout the liturgical
year. They are the events of Christ's life, which we are invited to ex-

perience within the context of our own history. The power of these mysteries of faith unfolds in our lives and becomes enfleshed in us, just as it was enfleshed in the humanity of Christ.

St. Paul refers to this when he writes: "In my own flesh I fill up what is lacking in the sufferings of Christ for the sake of his body, the church. I became a minister of this church . . . to preach among you his word in its fullness, that *mystery hidden* from ages past but now revealed to his holy ones" (Col 1:24-26, italics added).

Holy Week is the celebration of the Passover mystery. It is more than a recollection of the historical event of Passover, when the angel of death passed over the dwellings of the Israelites, sparing their first-born males from the plague of death decreed for the firstborn sons of the Egyptians. It is more than a recollection of Christ's sufferings, death, and resurrection. We remember these mysteries of faith because these same sacred events are meant to be relived and experienced in the historical circumstances of our own lives. We fill up and enflesh the hidden meaning of Christ's redemption as it seeks to be unfolded and revealed in our history.

Christ dwells within us and is ready to offer to the Father the gift of ourselves. There is no more need to offer the sacrifices of animals. The sacrifice of Christ offered once on the cross is relivable in the lives of each generation. The power of Christ's cross can be discerned and experienced within the context of our own sufferings and dyings. Christ suffered, died, and was raised from the dead to be in solidarity with the humanity and the sufferings of all. His sacrifice made possible our redemption, and he invites us to offer him our suffering humanity so that we might experience the mystery of his redemption. The celebration of this sacrifice, once offered on Calvary and now renewed in us, gives meaning to the sacrifice of the Eucharist.

If conversion has graced us to pass over from the world's illusions of grandeur to a life of grace, peace, and mercy, then we have truly shared in the sacrifice of Christ the high priest, who offers to his Father the gift of holiness indelibly sealed on our transformed humanity. Having died to sin, we are raised up by the Father to become the holiness of Jesus. Our vocation to be holy is fully realized when we turn over our sufferings to Christ so that the Father might raise him up in us. Holy Week is the remembrance of the mystery of Christ's death and resurrection, inviting us to allow this same mystery to be relived in our own dyings and risings.

Writing in his journal, Dag Hammarskjold has this to say about himself:

> You told yourself you would accept the decision of fate. But you lost your nerve when you discovered what this would require of you: then you realized how attached you still were to the world which has made you what you were, but which you would now have to leave behind. It felt like an amputation, a "little death," and you even listened to those voices which insinuated that you were deceiving yourself out of ambition. You will have to give up everything. Why, then, weep at this little death? Take it to you—quickly—with a smile die to this death, and become free to go further—one with your task, whole in your duty of the moment.[29]

QUESTIONS FOR YOUR REFLECTION

1. St. Paul writes: "If I must boast, I will make a point of my weaknesses" (2 Cor 11:30). In what way is your sufferings your "boast"?

2. In another place, St. Paul remarks that when we are weak we are also strong (see 2 Cor 12:10). What does St. Paul mean by that remark?

3. When people regard their sufferings as an integral part of Christ's ongoing renewal of the paschal mystery, does not the celebration of the Eucharist become a much more joyful experience? Is it true that the power of the Eucharist may not be experienced when people regard suffering as outside of God's plan of redemption and salvation for each of us?

4. Recall an experience when, at a moment of weakness, you demonstrated strength that amazed you when you reflected on the experience. Do you recall saying something like this: "It is a mystery to me how I did it!"

Humanity, Not Palms, Gives Glory to God

WORD

"In his humility Christ entered the dark regions of our fallen world and he is glad that he became humble for our sake, glad that he came and lived among us and shared in our nature in order to raise us up again to himself.

"So let us spread before his feet, not garments or soulless olive branches, which delight the eye for a few hours and then wither, but ourselves, clothed in his grace, or rather, clothed completely in him. We who have been baptized into Christ must ourselves be the garments that we spread before him. Let our souls take the place of the welcoming branches as we join today in the children's holy song: 'Blessed is he who comes in the name of the Lord. Blessed is the King of Israel'" (St. Andrew of Crete, bishop).[30]

REFLECTION

Holy Week begins with betrayal. The Gospel readings for the eucharistic celebrations of the first three days of Holy Week are about Judas and his unfaithfulness.

Faithfulness is a word that occurs many times in both Old and New Testaments. Our use of the word is very often not consistent with its biblical usage. While we might employ the word to mean endurance, perseverance, loyalty, or "hanging in there," the biblical meaning of faithfulness is fidelity to the truth.

The faithful person is one who, above all, has faith in the truth of his or her identity. That is what humility is. Humility does not mean self-denigration. Those who vilify themselves as evidence of their humility are unfaithful both to themselves and to God because they refuse to pursue the vocation of human growth and development. God did not create any of us to be the divine essence. Only God is divine.

111

God created us—called us—to be human creatures that we might develop the God-given capacity to share divine life. Without faithfulness to one's humanity and its creaturehood, there cannot be faithfulness to God's call to share divine life.

We sin against our creaturehood when our lives become foolish attempts to compete with God's creatorship. We become like God only when we acknowledge the lordship of the creator, who created and graced us to be the children of God. Christ was humble because he was faithful to the love and the reverence of his Father for our fallen humanity. "In his humility Christ entered the dark regions of our fallen world and he is glad that he became humble for our sake, glad that he came and lived among us and shared in our nature in order to raise us up to himself" (see "Word" above).

Judas betrayed Christ because he first betrayed his own identity for thirty pieces of silver. Judas had surrendered himself to the lordship of thirty pieces of silver. Having betrayed himself, he found it easy to betray Jesus. In the eyes of God, divine life garmented with human life is worth infinitely more than thirty pieces of silver.

What did the death of Jesus really represent? It represented a victory over the false promise that created things can provide us with worth. How paltry were the garments and palm branches people offered to Jesus on Palm Sunday! They were as useless and futile as the blood of bulls and calves. What Jesus longed for were the garments of their authentic humanity and the branches of praise and thanksgiving.

Jesus died so that he might expose the false representations alleged by Satan who dwells "in the dark regions of our fallen world." Jesus knew that nothing of this dark world had the power and strength to sustain him against the satanic hatred eager to see him crucified. Jesus entered the dark regions of this fallen world so that the Father's lordship might raise him and all humanity to the realms of light and life. Jesus handed over Satan's lie to the power of death so that the Father might hand on to humanity the power of God's creative life, putting death to death and giving life to life.

Christ, clothed in the garment of our humanity, is the will of the Father. It is likewise God's will that we be garmented with Christ. We gather at the Eucharist, garmented with Christ, to celebrate the worth of our graced and redeemed identity. We praise and thank God for a worth not measured by the worth of thirty pieces of silver. Rather, we gather to celebrate the unspeakable good news that our humanity is clothed with the fullness of Jesus Christ. It is that humanity that gives glory to God.

QUESTIONS FOR YOUR REFLECTION

1. No tree displays more grandeur and majesty than the palm tree. Yet its branches crumble more quickly than the severed branches of other trees. What does this contrast of the majesty and corruptibility of palm trees say to us on Palm Sunday?

2. When all is said and done, what is the identity common to all human beings, without exception (see Gen 1:26-27)? Why is this common identity an indictment against racism?

3. Why is faithfulness to one's true identity a guarantee that it will last forever?

4. Why is humanity a better garment for Christ's glory than the majesty and beauty of palms or, for that matter, of any other earthly good?

We Have Something God Doesn't

WORD

"Who is Christ if not the Word of God. . . ? He had no power of himself to die for us: he had to take from us our mortal flesh. This was the way in which, though immortal, he was able to die; the way in which he chose to give life to mortal men: he would first share with us, and then enable us to share with him. Of ourselves we had no power to live, nor did he of himself have the power to die.

"Accordingly, he effected a wonderful exchange with us, through mutual sharing: we gave him the power to die, he will give us the power to live.

"The death of the Lord our God should not be a cause of shame for us; rather, it should be our greatest hope, our greatest glory. In taking upon himself the death that he found in us, he has faithfully promised to give us life in him, such as we cannot have of ourselves" (St. Augustine, bishop).[31]

REFLECTION

Christ's resurrection offered humanity God's way of surviving death; Christ's death offered God humanity's way of achieving resurrection. In exchange for his gift of life, God needed from us our gift of death. For life, God asks of us death; in exchange for death, we ask of God life.

God is life itself. God did not know how to die. Only death stood between God's gift of himself and our sharing in eternal life. "We gave him the power to die [so that he could] give us the power to live" (see "Word" above). We gave God Good Friday. In exchange God gave us Easter Sunday.

As each of us needs the gift of resurrection, so Christ needs our gift of death. Until each of us offers to God our own unique way of dying, we prevent God from raising up Christ in our unique capacity to share his resurrection. God longs to experience death in the unique way each of us experiences the many dyings that mark our lives on earth.

114

One of the reasons why we fear to embrace death is that we fear to embrace resurrection. Death means letting go of what we can control. Death appears to be final. That appearance wrests from us our control of both past and present. It demands the radical surrender of any identity with which this world has defined us. The death God begs of us is the abdication and the abandonment of any trace of identity we have derived from this world's promises. We fear death not because we deny a life after death but because we have not the slightest hint of what its fullest personal experience is. Death reveals the futility of trying to define God's gift of eternal life by the criteria this world offers.

God does not forsake us in death. What God forsakes are this world's empty promises. Death is clear testimony that this world's promises cannot save us from death. Where are the world's promises as we lay dying? Which of the world's creatures stands ready to guide us across the line from death to eternal life? Can anyone name one reality, material or immaterial, that has the capacity of providing eternal identity? What created good can possibly raise us up to an identity exceeding our physical and mental capacities to see and hear? And if nothing of this world can lead from death into eternal life, does human existence, then, have any meaning? Are we worth no more than that which we can have, buy, and control?

> Woe to him who says to wood, "Awake!"
>   to dumb stone, "Arise!"
>   Can such a thing give oracles?
> See, it is overlaid with gold and silver,
>   but there is no life breath in it.
> Of what avail is the carved image
>   that its maker should carve it?
> Or the molten image and lying oracle,
>   that its very maker should trust in it,
>   and make dumb idols?
> But the LORD is in his holy temple;
>   silence before him, all the earth! (Hab 2:19-20)

We await death with hope not because death ushers us into eternity on the basis of our earthly experiences but because hope promises an identity infinitely beyond the ambience of our imagination. How can hope be hope when what it promises is within the purview of our understanding and control? Hope is hope because of the integrity of the one who promises. "Take my word for it" is the credential of those who solicit another's trust. "Take my Word for it" is precisely what God the Father asks of us. God gave us the Word that the identity we were created to become in Christ might be realized. God's Word became flesh and spent his lifetime dying so that his Father might raise us up to an eternal lifetime of living.

QUESTIONS FOR YOUR REFLECTION

1. In what sense is resistance to dying also resistance to a life and a goodness that transcends any life and goodness found here upon earth?

2. Jesus cried out on the cross: "My God, my God, why have you forsaken me?" (Mark 15:34) What must be forsaken and be put to death in us if we are to embrace the fullness of our humanity's resurrection in Christ?

3. There is an old saying about the world's wealth: "You can't take it with you." Reaching all the way back to the first chapter of Genesis, what can you discover that clearly indicates what each of us can take with us after death?

4. We die again and again on this earth so that we can be born again and again on this earth. But the last time we die will also be the last time we are born again. What are your thoughts about this?

Discipline Makes Room for Christ

WORD

> *"At the time it is administered, all discipline seems a cause for grief and not for joy, but later it brings forth the fruit of peace and justice to those who are trained in its school"* (Heb 12:11).

REFLECTION

One is not more disciplined simply because one has endured more punishment. Any discipline gained from punishment is nothing more than behavior modification. Authentic discipline is not primarily concerned with behavior modification. Discipline develops the capacity for renewed personhood with a new center focus. Whatever is the center of our lives will determine our behavior.

There is distance between the admiration of an ideal and its integration into personhood. Ideals easily appreciated and admired become our identity only with great difficulty. The hardship to become what we appreciate lies in the process of rearranging our lives around a new center that we have decided is worth the effort of a new configuration. The journey from repentance to conversion is grueling. Pulling away from the configuring magnetic field of this world's spirit to the configuring magnetism of Christ's life demands of us an unrelenting and never-ceasing determination to become the fruit of the new configuration. One may dream, for example, of becoming a champion. Without discipline, however, the most one can expect is the prospect of becoming a champion dreamer. When dreams are at the center, the dreamer will behave like a dreamer.

In baptism we are called to more than aspiration. We are called to the fulfillment of God's plan, and we are offered the vision of Christ-likeness. Christ became our image and likeness because we were created in God's image and likeness. Our humanity became the center of Christ's earthly existence just as Christ became the center of our existence.

117

Jesus embraced the discipline of the cross so that human nature might be restored to its original purpose and plan. Christ was sent to draw us to the Father. Our response to his magnetism implies a brand-new configuration of life patterns around Christ, who came as God's magnetic field. In this field, Christ calls us to revolve our lives around his way, his truth, and his life.

Repentance is the decision to opt for these new patterns. Holiness of life takes form when there is a consistency between longing and achievement. It is not enough to long for a new center in one's life. If repentance is the decision to arrange one's life around a new magnetic center, then conversion, with its discipline, is the day-by-day process whereby patterns of living are rearranged and the aspirations of baptism become a reality.

St. Paul writes: "Are you not aware that we who were baptized into Christ Jesus were baptized into his death? . . . If we have been united with him through likeness to his death, so shall we be through a like resurrection" (Rom 6:3-5). It is not enough to begin with the virtues of Christ's resurrection. To be holy there must also be evidence that our identities bear the marks of Christ's cross. It is by way of the cross that we give evidence that we have made a clean break with a pattern of living derived from the spirit of the world. If this clean break has not even been attempted, we become stumbling blocks to God's work of conversion and resurrection. A resurrection holiness without the discipline of the cross is no more than a mask of holiness.

Our unique role in God's work of holiness is to "proclaim the death of the Lord until he comes" (1 Cor 11:26). Our own Passover, which we celebrate this Holy Week, is passage from a former way of living to a new, from an old center to a new. God promised to raise us up to the new. It is our responsibility to break the hold of the old. That takes discipline.

QUESTIONS FOR YOUR REFLECTION

1. Discipline is not an end in itself. What is the goal of discipline?

2. Somewhere I read: "The purpose of discipline is to create within us the space God needs to exercise God's freedom to make us holy." When discipline is practiced for the sake of discipline, how is its purpose nullified?

3. Repentance is the decision to opt for new patterns of living. Patterns do not develop unless there is a center around which they configure. If Christ is to become the center of our lives, our source of holiness, in what sense do our lives "proclaim the death of the Lord until he comes" (1 Cor 11:26)?

4. When the discipline of ascetical exercises rather than Christ comes to be regarded as the center of holiness, isn't it really idolatry that has become the center of our lives?

WEDNESDAY OF HOLY WEEK

Poverty of Spirit Enables Christ to Be Life's Centerpiece

WORD

"Strive for peace with all . . . , and for that holiness without which no one can see the Lord" (Heb 12:14).

REFLECTION

We cannot relate without a point of reference. Communication is extremely difficult without analogy. No one realized this more than Jesus. He used the words "like" and "as" to describe the kingdom of heaven. For Jesus, his Father's lordship was the magnetic field around which he centered his own human life. What others considered as ultimate and, therefore, unrelatable to the Father had little meaning for Jesus.

Jesus easily related all of creation to the reign of God. In his parables, he used God's creatures as the frame of reference to teach the meaning of God's reign. For Jesus, God's kingdom was like a good Samaritan, a master who trusted his stewards, a lost coin, a lost sheep, a pearl of great price, a generous master who paid those hired last the same wages as those hired first, a mustard seed, salt, light, thorns, fig trees, and a repentant young man who, in a pigpen, decided that back at his father's house he never had it so good.

119

From God's point of view, Jesus offered the totality of God's sovereignty as the measure and the point of reference for a love marking "out for us the fullness of love that we ought to have for one another" (St. Augustine, bishop).[32] For Jesus, the totality of his response to the Father turned out to be death on a cross.

While the shedding of blood is one sign of total love, it is by no means the only sign of total love. St. John writes: "As Christ laid down his life for us, so we ought to lay down our lives for [others]" (1 John 3:16). John's comparison of Christ shedding his blood is not his sine qua non prescription for the model of total love. John refers to a totality of love Jesus was able to witness because the Father was at the center of his life. When Jesus is the central truth of our lives, we, too, have the capacity to love as totally as God loved Jesus and as God loves us.

The perfection of love cannot be set within the parameters of any specific manner of total loving, even death by martyrdom. El Salvador's Archbishop Oscar Romero shed his blood as a witness of the total love he felt for all of his people. Mother Theresa of Calcutta likewise witnesses the totality of her love for human dignity but has not shed her blood. Both are martyrs because both witness to total love.

Jesus died on the cross not to specify crucifixion as *the* way to exercise the capacity to love but to reveal the unique capacity of loving that each of us possesses. Love's totality is measured by the fullness of God's lordship, which we have enthroned at the center of our lives. That lordship is our point of reference. The perfection of our love is measured by the totality with which we empty ourselves of the sovereignty we have attributed to our possessions and strengths. St. Paul puts it this way: "Those things I used to consider gain I have now reappraised as loss in the light of Christ. I have come to rate all as loss in the light of the surpassing knowledge of my Lord Jesus Christ" (Phil 3:7-8).

Total surrender is not marked by mere verbal renunciation of God's gifts. Rather, it is marked by the recognition that God measures holiness by our willingness to be poor in spirit. What curbs God's freedom to make us holy are the sovereignties we enthrone at the center of our own capacities to love. That is why Jesus was moved to exclaim, "Blessed are the poor in spirit" (Matt 5:3).

Holiness is not something God gives us in exchange for somethings we give back to God. Holiness is the full and total reign of Christ's presence forming and shaping who we are in the poverty of spirit we have chosen as our way of living. That spirit enables God to love us more freely and frees us to say "amen" more fully to that love. Why? Because no other sovereignty stands in the way. God calls for a poverty of spirit that lets go of any earthbound sovereignty reigning in our lives. We can witness the holiness of Christ's presence because, in the spirit of poverty, we have been able to understand what St. Paul means when he writes: "Jesus Christ is Lord!" (Phil 2:11)

QUESTIONS FOR YOUR REFLECTION

1. When Jesus shed his blood, his death on the cross presented a model and witness of total love. What does the word "martyr" mean? Is shedding our blood a must in order for us to qualify as witnesses of total love?

2. We can be saved only to the extent that God is free to live and work within us. What is the relationship between God's freedom and our freedom to choose a life poor in spirit?

3. The poor in spirit are not limited to those who either have been dispossessed of this world's possessions or have vowed to be dispossessed of them. To be poor in spirit means to dispossess ourselves of the sovereignty we have attributed to our possessions. How do those who vow poverty demonstrate that poverty in spirit is possible and attractive? Can those who vow poverty be signs of encouragement for those who wonder what "poor in spirit" means?

4. Jesus warned that "none of those who cry out, 'Lord, Lord,' will enter the kingdom of God" (Matt 7:21). How does poverty in spirit enable us to understand more fully what the lordship of Jesus means?

Obedience Is Not Subservience

WORD

"Son though he was, he learned obedience from what he suffered; and when perfected, he became the source of eternal salvation for all who obey him" (Heb 5:8-9).

REFLECTION

In a democratic society obedience is an unpopular word. Too often, "obedience" and "subservience" share the same meaning. Subservience, however, is not a synonym for obedience. Obedience is a human response because its authority calls for human development. Uppermost in the intent of those who call for obedience is their reverence for human dignity. Uppermost in the intent of those who call for subservience is the task done rather than dignity revered. Subservience is not a human response, nor do authoritarians want it to be human.

Obedience never places task ahead of personhood. Authorities who have a right to obedience never forget their duty to place the achievement of task within the context of its relationship to human dignity. Authoritarianism, however, places human dignity at the disposal of production and its marketability. Such vulgarity is cancerous to the soul of society itself.

Fidelity to human dignity characterized the obedience of Jesus. Even though he took on the form of a slave, he refused subservience to religious observances that either ignored human dignity or placed it on the periphery of its sacred meaning and purpose. For example, the Sabbath, he insisted, served the human person, not otherwise. His passion to liberate human dignity revealed Jesus as radically different, and for that difference he suffered and died. But Jesus never became embittered. His sufferings only served to magnify the fullest meaning of the mission he was sent to accomplish.

When Pilate asked Jesus, "What have you done?" Jesus answered:

"My kingdom does not belong to this world.
If my kingdom were of this world,

my subjects would be fighting
to save me from being handed over to the Jews.
As it is, my kingdom is not here" (John 18:35-36).

The obedience of Jesus called him away from servitude to alleged sovereignties that defined humanity by the task gods of authoritarianism. The alienation that Jesus was forced to suffer in turn freed him to examine more closely the ever-widening circle of authentic human identity and its connection to humanity's ultimate purpose. Christ's sufferings taught him an obedience whereby humanity might define itself according to a new solidarity, rearranging all the patterns of living around a new center.

God calls us away from the freedom to have so that we might pursue the freedom to be. The sufferings of Jesus laid bare the meaninglessness of all world-defined measurements of human identity. We are not defined by what we own or what we possess. If we are, then we are free to *be* only to the extent that we have license to own. The sufferings and death of Jesus enabled all of humanity to be redefined and re-owned by God who created us to *be* in the image and likeness of God. That is how we *be!*

We were redefined by Christ's sufferings and death not by way of subservience to a taskmaster but by way of obedience to a loving Father calling us to discover an authentic relationship that transcends human servility. The obedience of Jesus reveals that we belong to God because absolutely nothing of this world revealed a capacity to rescue Jesus from his sufferings and death on the cross. The serpent's boast to Adam and Eve, "you certainly will not die" (Gen 3:4) because of the forbidden fruit he invited them to eat was a lie! God, not a creature of God's making, raised up Jesus, and it is in Christ that all of humanity is raised up by God. God's fidelity to a betrayed humanity reveals the ultimate belonging of every human being.

"Religion" is to be relinked both to God and to one another. Nothing of this world, however sacred, has the power and the sovereignty to identify us as righteous and just. We are made right and just because we have been freed to obey the call of God to be God's own. God created us to be like God. This is our belonging. Any other linking with lesser gods as the justifying and ultimate reason for human existence can never satisfy the longings that lie deep in the mystery of our lives. In that mystery we find the moreness of human identity only God can call forth. Obedience is the glad embrace of that unrealized identity.

The death of Jesus on the cross was perfect obedience. His task of dying was a not subservient response to an angry God seeking the appeasement of an injured sense of righteousness. Rather, Jesus heard the Father's call to be the servant through whose obedience humankind could become re-owned and relinked to God and one another by bonds of the divine identity that give meaning to our existence. We exist because God created us to be in his image and likeness. All other worldly claims offering ultimate belonging subject God's beautiful creation to futility.

QUESTIONS FOR YOUR REFLECTION

1. At the Last Supper, Jesus said to the Twelve, "Do this in remembrance of me" (1 Cor 11:24). Is this an imperative to perform a task? Is Jesus requiring subservience, or are his words well within the context of obedience?

2. St. John does not describe the Last Supper as do either the other evangelists or St. Paul. Rather, St. John describes Christ's action of washing the feet of the Twelve during the meal. Does the significance of Christ's washing the feet of his disciples during the meal have eucharistic meaning? What is the meaning of Eucharist in terms of each Christian's daily lifestyle?

3. If the celebration of Eucharist signifies a human existence wherein human dignity is defined by its relationship with God, can the obligation to participate in each Sunday's eucharistic ritual be justified? Is being physically present at Sunday Mass all that we are obligated to?

In Touch with Christ's Blood Today

WORD

> "For if the blood of goats and bulls and the sprinkling of a heifer's ashes can sanctify those who are defiled so that their flesh is cleansed, how much more will the blood of Christ, who through the eternal spirit offered himself up unblemished to God, cleanse our consciences from dead works to worship the living God!" (Heb 9:13-14)

> "In those days, when the destroying angel saw the blood [of the lamb] on the doors he did not dare to enter, so how much less will the devil approach now when he sees, not that figurative blood on the doors, but the true blood on the lips of believers, the doors of the temple of Christ" (St. John Chrysostom, bishop).[33]

REFLECTION

On the cross Christ shed his blood once and for all.

> As high priest of the good things which have come to be, he entered once for all into the sanctuary, passing through the greater and more perfect tabernacle not made by hands, that is, not belonging to this creation. He entered, not with the blood of goats and calves, but with his own blood, and achieved eternal redemption (Heb 9:11-12).

How do we make contact with the saving blood of Christ, offered in sacrifice twenty centuries ago? How are we cleansed and purified of our sins today by the precious blood of Jesus? In what sense does the blood of Jesus, shed two thousand years ago, force Satan to back away from those who touch to their lips the saving blood of the Son of God?

It was not necessary for Jesus, so to speak, to spill his blood over and over as prescribed for sacrifices of the Jewish Law. When Jesus spilled his blood on the cross, he became the font of the never-ending river of his Father's Word. Jesus, the Word of God, was raised up by God as the life-giving principle for all generations until the end of time. When God sent the Holy Spirit into the world, the power and presence of God's Word, ever the life-giving principle for God's people, filled the whole earth and made that saving Word forever available.

For all time, those who listen to God's Word make contact with the blood of Jesus. Just as Jesus' blood was the life-giving principle of his human body for the humanity of all, so Jesus, God's Word, became the life-giving principle of the Church, which in time and space is the sacred body of Christ. This encounter with the Word of God is signified and celebrated each time we sacramentally eat of Christ's flesh and drink his blood, which we share in the sacramental celebration of the Holy Eucharist. When we drink from the cup of Christ's sacramental blood, we bear witness to the joyful truth that God's Word both forms and shares our identity. The Eucharist becomes a powerful sign celebrating our belief that the Word of God, dwelling within us, has become our own life-giving principal coursing through Christ's body, the Church.

In the Eucharist we proclaim that, just as the sacramental presence of Christ's blood nourishes us and becomes a part of us, so the Word of God nourishes us and shares our identity. It is this identity of Christ, forming and transforming our humanity, that prevents Satan from being effective in our lives. He shrinks back from lips purpled with the sacrament of Christ's precious blood because he fears the character of Christ's Word, coloring the character of God's people.

The Eucharist and the Word it proclaims is the never-ending celebration of that once-for-all gift of Christ's precious blood. "Eucharist" means "good gift," and it was Christ's gift of his life poured out that became the event Christians call "Good," namely, the Friday Christ shed his blood. The goodness of this day sanctifies every day and makes all of our days filled with the holiness of God. Each day of our lives is stamped with the Word of God's life-giving promise of salvation. The world is charged with the power and the presence of this Word. As the sacred writer says:

> [God's Word] "is not up in the sky, that you should say, 'Who will go up in the sky to get it for us and tell us of it, that we may carry it out?' Nor is it across the sea, that you should say, 'Who will cross the sea to get it for us and tell us of it, that we may carry it out?' No, it is something very near to you, already in your mouths and in your hearts; you have only to carry it out" (Deut 30:12-14).

QUESTIONS FOR YOUR REFLECTION

1. In what way does the Word of God stand as a sacred collateral, making credible the real presence of Christ's sacramental presence? Can you offer evidence that, since the Second Vatican Council, the place of the Word of God in sacred liturgy has been significantly enhanced?

2. In light of the reflection, how would you explain that the Word of God enables us to be in touch with the blood of Christ?

3. Why must every celebration of the Eucharist include both Word and sign? What happens to worship's authenticity when the Word of God is the weakest part of the liturgy service, while devotion and reverence to the sacred signs of worship get the worshipers' preoccupation? Conversely, what is the danger to worship's authenticity when worshipers are preoccupied solely with the ministry of the Word?

4. Why was it unnecessary for the Son of God to shed his blood more than once?

5. What is "Good" about "Good Friday"?

A Day Whose Emptiness Is the Promise of Fullness

WORD

"While the promise of entrance into his rest still holds, we ought to be fearful of disobeying lest any of you be judged to have lost his chance of entering. We have indeed heard the good news, as they did. But the word which they heard did not profit them, for they did not receive it in faith. It is we who have believed who enter into that rest" (Heb 4:1-3).

"Rise, let us leave this place. The enemy led you out of the earthly paradise. I will not restore you to that paradise, but I will enthrone you in heaven. I forbade you the tree that was only a symbol of life, but see, I who am life itself am now one with you" ("An Ancient Homily on Holy Saturday").[34]

REFLECTION

There is an emptiness that marks Holy Saturday. We enter our churches where our eyes gaze at tabernacles whose open doors reveal the absence of the sacramental presence of Christ. Like the gaping mouths of the dead, these empty tabernacles seem to mock the sacred name "Emmanuel," "God is with us." Yet these open doors invite us to follow the Savior as he "descended into hell" on the mission of redemption for those who, since death, had dwelt beyond the boundaries of this world. Today we remember that he who spent three years of public ministry among the living proclaiming the good news of salvation spent three days among the dead summoning them to a place of rest no longer barricaded by death.

Holy Saturday invites us to experience symbolically what it would be like to experience human life without Christ who is our faith and hope. For this one day we share a darkness with our first parents and all of our brothers and sisters who dwelt between earth and heaven,

128

untouched by the grace of the incarnation and the hope it offered those who were given the opportunity to believe in Christ.

What a blessing the gift of faith! How necessary for us to descend with Christ, at least for this one Saturday each year, into the scary regions of broken solidarity! How blessed to stand with Christ, who is the fruit of God's promise, to see the harvest reaped by Adam and Eve as they endeavored to usurp the fruits of a communion that only God's lordship can provide. We stand with Christ at the threshold of this place of waiting, where unenfleshed hope had been no more than the faint remembrance of a promise made "in the beginning."

What a blessing for us to hear Christ, the incarnation of God's primeval promise of salvation, cry out: "Rise, let us leave this place. The enemy led you out of the earthly paradise . . . , I will enthrone you in heaven" (see "Word" above).

Today, what we hear from the lips of Christ as he "descended into hell" we hear daily from the lips of the Church as she calls us to soar on the wings of faith and hope. The voice of Holy Saturday's entombed Christ speaking the good news of liberation to countless generations of the dead is also the voice of the risen Christ speaking to us through the Church's liberating message of salvation: "Rise, let us leave this place" of doubt and uncertainty. Come the dawn that signals the end of this dark, desert day of Christ's holy absence, the celebration of the Easter mystery will again fill these empty temples with alleluia choruses, while tabernacle doors, closed once again, will quietly announce that Christ dwells among us. He who has been our Lenten companion as we journeyed toward his crucifixion now becomes our Easter companion as we journey with burning hearts to Emmaus, where we believe that we shall recognize him in the breaking of the bread.

QUESTIONS FOR YOUR REFLECTION

1. In the context of a frequent remark, "Life holds no meaning for me," what does "meaning" mean? Is there a connection between meaninglessness and emptiness?

2. Sometimes meaninglessness and emptiness suggest suicide. Rather than despair as the fruit of either, don't times of meaninglessness and emptiness provide a readying time for the liberating message of Jesus? In what way do these examples of a limbo existence here upon earth, when sustained by the virtues of faith and hope, reveal their authentic meaning?

3. The presence of Christ is not confined to the sacramental presence of Christ in church tabernacles. The whole world is the tabernacle of the risen Christ. Nevertheless, in what way does the tabernacle presence of Christ support our faith in Christ's risen presence everywhere in the universe?

Holy Saturday, Easter Sunday: Two Prisms for Baptism

WORD

> *"Are you not aware that we who were baptized into Christ Jesus were baptized into his death? Through baptism into his death we were buried with him, so that, just as Christ was raised from the dead by the glory of the Father, we too might live a new life"* (Rom 6:3-4).

REFLECTION

A Holy Saturday reading at the liturgy of the Eucharist and an Easter Sunday reading from the Church's Liturgy of the Hours present two prisms through which baptism can be more clearly understood. For all who gather to celebrate the sacrament of baptism, the Holy Saturday liturgy is the joyful climax of the repentance to which Ash Wednesday challenged them: "Turn away from sin and be faithful to the Gospel" (Ash Wednesday liturgy).

On Ash Wednesday we are challenged to spend the season of Lent reflecting on baptism's invitation that we place Jesus Christ at the center of our lives so that we might radiate and proclaim Christ's attitudes, values, and priorities. Always present throughout Lent is baptism's imperative that followers of Christ die with Christ in order to be raised with him. To the extent that this is the repentant intent of those who bow to receive the ashes of Lent's first day, Holy Saturday is truly a joyful celebration of baptism's call to repentance.

Easter Sunday is also a celebration of baptism, but baptism seen through the prism of the lived reality of our repentance. The Liturgy of the Hours repeats St. Paul's striking challenge to the Romans: "Are you not aware that we who were baptized into Christ Jesus were baptized into his death?" (see "Word" above) The voice of the Church invites us, at prayer, to consider deeply the full implications of what the Church celebrates with joy at the Holy Saturday eucharistic liturgy: What might be some of the implications of St. Paul's challenge? Do we fully realize the lived reality of baptism's sacramentality? Are we aware of baptism's imperative that we place Jesus Christ at the center of our lives? Are we aware of the profound change that this imperative demands of the way we live? Do we understand with joy how the Church will come to be perceived when what we say we believe becomes the way we live?

Holy Saturday and Easter Sunday have this in common: both share the reality of Christ at the center of Christian living. Be that as it may, both do not share the same prism. Repentance is a profound change of mind. Conversion is a profound change of heart. When repentance journeys to the heart, there takes place a change of life. Repentance cries out, "I meant what I said!" Conversion cries out, "I have become what I meant!" When the prisms of repentance and conversion are joined in marriage, baptism's imperative will have been given birth: Christ, the center of our lives!

Are we really aware, then, of the implications of being baptized into Christ's death? St. Paul is not telling us to be aware of the necessity of dying by way of an act of fatal violence against human life. But baptism does call us to die to a way of living that gives evidence that our minds and hearts may have been delivered over to violent lordships that occupy the centrality of our lives. Baptism calls us to die to attitudes, values, and priorities that do violence to human dignity and the justice that allows human dignity to grow, develop, and mature.

The specific way Christ died as the criterion for discipleship is not what St. Paul calls us to be aware of. Rather, he calls us to be aware that Christ's death was an indignity paid to human dignity, the indignity of the violence that erupts from those whose center of existence is "I." Violence to human dignity and justice is often the response of those whose ego-centrality is confronted by those whose Christ-centrality is the meaning of existence. For Jesus, the center of his life was the Father. Jesus' way, truth, and life was the visible, tangible, and concrete embodiment of his Father's will and identity. "Whoever has seen me has seen the Father. How can you say, 'Show us the Father'?" (see John 14:9) The reason Jesus died at the hands of violence to human dignity was that human dignity has no defense except the Father who created it. God's reason for our existence is resurrection!

The joy of Easter is this: The resurrection of Jesus is God's means of proclaiming the dignity of human existence. The resurrection of Jesus was heaven's response to a violence that poverty of spirit has not the capacity to combat. The lifeless body of Christ on the cross was grim witness to humanity's incapacity to justify with earthly means humankind's divine purpose. Jesus died on the cross to reveal the emptiness of the serpent's lie that egocentricity is the centerpiece of human existence. When God raised up Jesus, that lie died. It's serpentine designer has been crawling ever since.

We rejoice on Easter Sunday because our fidelity to Christ crucified and Christ risen as the center of our lives has become the hope that in the crucifixions of our daily lives the Father has also raised us up. The resurrection of Christ stands as the lasting confirmation of God's unimaginable and indescribable love for creatures created in the image and likeness of God. Baptism is a once-for-all celebration of Christ's resurrection. Repentance is our admission that the centrality of that resurrection—its hope a certainty—is yet to be realized in us.

Are we aware of the implications of dying and rising with Christ? Isn't death to shallow reasons of egocentricity worth suffering when, with Mary Magdalene, we stand at Christ's empty tomb? Is the burden of repentance and conversion to which baptism invites us not worth the indescribable joy of hearing Mary Magdalene say, "The Lord has been taken from the tomb"? If we have the faith to embrace the burdens of repentance and conversion, then surely Easter "is the day the Lord has made; let us be glad and rejoice in it!" (Ps 118:24)

QUESTIONS FOR YOUR REFLECTION

1. The word "repentance" does not mean punishment. It means renewal. If baptism is a once-for-all call for renewal, in what sense is repentance baptism revisited?

2. The spectacle of empty pews on Easter Monday is commentary to the allegation that Catholics view Lent as an end in itself and Easter as the end of Lent. What is your reflection on this?

3. It has been said that every Sunday is "little Easter." What does this mean? Isn't this true of every eucharistic celebration? Isn't it also true that Lent is an integral part of every eucharistic celebration?

4. The paschal mystery, Christ's death and resurrection, is at the heart of Catholic faith. How would you explain the contention that the paschal mystery is the way, the truth, and the life of human existence? Do you see the connection between our assent that Christ is at the center of human life and our consent to make his paschal mystery the basis for our human behavior and lifestyle?

Notes

1. St. Leo the Great, "Lenten Sermon 6," *Patrologia Graeca*. See *Liturgy of the Hours* (New York: Catholic Book Publishing Company, 1976) 2:60.

2. St. John Chrysostom, "Homily 6," *Patrologia Graeca*. See *Liturgy of the Hours* 2:69.

3. St. Augustine, "Commentary on the Psalms," *Corpus Christianorum Series Latina*. See *Liturgy of the Hours* 2:87.

4. Ibid.

5. *The Documents of Vatican II, The Church Today,* Walter M. Abbott, ed. (New York: The America Press, 1966) no. 32.

6. St. Gregory Nazianzen, "Discourse 14," *Patrologia Graeca*. See *Liturgy of the Hours* 2:97.

7. Aphraates, "A Demonstration," *Patrologia Syriaca*. See *Liturgy of the Hours* 2:113-114.

8. St. Aelred, "The Mirror of Love," *Patrologia Latina*. See *Liturgy of the Hours* 2:131.

9. "Pastoral Constitution on the Church in the Modern World," nos. 9–10.

10. St. Augustine, "Commentary on the Psalms," *Corpus Christianorum Series Latina*. See *Liturgy of the Hours* 2:168.

11. The Dogmatic Constitution on the Church, no. 1, ed. Abbot.

12. Gerard Manley Hopkins, "God's Grandeur." See *Liturgy of the Hours* 1:1681.

13. St. Augustine, "Treatise on John," *Corpus Christianorum Series Latina*. See *Liturgy of the Hours* 2:212.

14. Anthony de Mello, *Song of the Bird* (Chicago: Loyola University Press, 1983) 124.

15. St. Peter Chrysologus, "Sermon 43," *Patrologia Latina*. See *Liturgy of the Hours* 2:231.

16. Tertullian, "On Prayer," *Corpus Christianorum Series Latina*. See *Liturgy of the Hours* 2:250.

17. St. Gregory the Great, "Moral Reflections on Job," *Patrologia Latina*. See *Liturgy of the Hours* 2:259.

18. St. Leo the Great, "Lenten Sermon 10," *Patrologia Latina*. See *Liturgy of the Hours* 2:295.

19. "Economic Justice for All," no. 24 (Washington: National Conference of Catholic Bishops, 1986) 332.

20. Hopkins, "God's Grandeur." See *Liturgy of the Hours* 1:1681.

21. "The Church in the Modern World," nos. 37–38.

22. "On Evangelization in the Modern World," no. 41 (Washington: Publications Office of the U.S. Catholic Conference, 1976) 28.

23. St. Leo the Great, "The Passion of the Lord," *Patrologia Latina*. See *Liturgy of the Hours* 2:358.

24. St. Augustine, "Commentary on the Psalms," *Corpus Christianorum Series Latina*. See *Liturgy of the Hours* 2:366.

25. Johann Baptist Metz, *The Emergent Church* (New York: The Crossroad Publishing Company, 1986) 1–2.

26. Ibid. 2.

27. The Dogmatic Constitution on the Church, no. 9, ed. Abbott.

28. St. Gregory Nazianzen, "Homily on Prayer," *Patrologia Graeca*. See *Liturgy of the Hours* 2:392.

29. Dag Hammarskjold, *Markings* (New York: Ballantine Books, 1964) 137.

30. St. Andrew of Crete, "Sermon on Prayer," *Patrologia Graeca*. See *Liturgy of the Hours* 2:419.

31. St. Augustine, "Sermo Guelferbytanus 3," *Supplementum Patrologiae Latinae*. See *Liturgy of the Hours* 2:432.

32. St. Augustine, "A Treatise on John," *Supplementum Patrologiae Latinae*. See *Liturgy of the Hours* 2:449.

33. St. John Chrysostom, "Catecheses," *Sources Chretiennes*. See *Liturgy of the Hours* 2:473.

34. "An Ancient Homily on Holy Saturday," *Patrologia Graeca*. See *Liturgy of the Hours* 2:498.